AQA Mathematics

for GCSE

Exclusively endorsed and approved by AQA

Series Editor
Paul Metcalf

Series Advisor
David Hodgson

Lead Author
Steven Lomax

June Haighton
Anne Haworth
Janice Johns
Andrew Manning
Kathryn Scott
Chris Sherrington
Margaret Thornton
Mark Willis

HIGHER
Module 3

™ Nelson Thornes
a Wolters Kluwer business

Published in 2006 by:
Nelson Thornes Ltd
Delta Place
27 Bath Road
CHELTENHAM
GL53 7TH
United Kingdom

06 07 08 09 10 / 10 9 8 7 6 5 4 3 2

A catalogue record for this book is available from the British Library.

ISBN 0 7487 9757 2

Cover photograph: Swan by Mark Hamblin/OSF/Photolibrary
Illustrations by Roger Penwill
Page make-up by MCS Publishing Services Ltd, Salisbury, Wiltshire

Printed in Great Britain by Scotprint

Acknowledgements

The authors and publishers wish to thank the following for their contribution:
David Bowles for providing the Assess questions
David Hodgson for reviewing draft manuscripts

Thank you to the following schools:
Little Heath School, Reading
The Kingswinford School, Dudley
Thorne Grammar School, Doncaster

The publishers thank the following for permission to reproduce copyright material:

Explore photos
Diver – Corel 55 (NT); Astronaut – Digital Vision 6 (NT);
Mountain climber – Digital Vision XA (NT); Desert explorer – Martin Harvey/Alamy.

Lighthouse – Corel 502 (NT); Solar System Montage – NASA; Stars in the Tarantula Nebula – NASA, The Hubble Heritage Team, STScl, AURA; Supermarket – Stockbyte 9 (NT); Concert hall – Digital Stock 13 (NT); Puppy – G/V Hart/Photodisc 50 (NT); Seagulls – Photodisc 6 (NT); Goldfish – Alex Homer; Duke on the Crater's Edge – NASA, John W. Young; An Ancient Storm in the Jovian Atmosphere – NASA, The Hubble Heritage Team, STScl, AURA, Amy Simon Cornell; Bacteria – Photodisc 72 (NT); House sale – Photodisc 76 (NT); Tiger – Nat Photos/Digital Vision AF (NT); Formula One car – Corel 231 (NT); Stained glass – Corel 153 (NT).

The publishers have made every effort to contact copyright holders but apologise if any have been overlooked.

Contents

Introduction

This book has been written by teachers and examiners who not only want you to get the best grade you can in your GCSE exam but also to enjoy maths.

Each chapter has the following stages:

OBJECTIVES

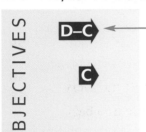

The objectives at the start of the chapter give you an idea of what you need to do to get each grade. Remember that the examiners expect you to perform well at the lower grade questions on the exam paper in order to get the higher grades. So, even if you are aiming for an A* grade you will still need to do well on the D grade questions on the exam paper.

Learn 1

Key information and examples to show you how to do each topic. There are several Learn sections in each chapter.

Apply 1

Questions that allow you to practise what you have just learned.

Means that these questions should be attempted with a calculator.

Means that these questions are practice for the non-calculator paper in the exam and should be attempted without a calculator.

Get Real! *These questions show how the maths in this topic can be used to solve real-life problems.*

<u>1</u> *Underlined questions are harder questions.*

Explore

Open-ended questions to extend what you have just learned. These are good practice for your coursework task.

ASSESS

End of chapter questions written by an examiner.

Some chapters feature additional questions taken from real past papers to further your understanding.

1 Integers

C **Examiners would normally expect students who get a C grade to be able to:**

Recognise prime numbers

Find the reciprocal of a number

Find the least common multiple (LCM) of two simple numbers

Find the highest common factor (HCF) of two simple numbers

Write a number as a product of prime factors

B **Examiners would normally expect students who get a B grade also to be able to:**

Find the least common multiple (LCM) of two or more numbers

Find the highest common factor (HCF) of two or more numbers

What you should already know ...

- Understand the four rules of number
- Understand place value
- Understand the inequality signs $<$, $>$, $\leqslant$ and $\geqslant$
- Know the meaning of 'sum' and 'product'

- Apply the four rules to positive and negative numbers
- Change a decimal into a fraction
- Change a mixed number into a top-heavy fraction

Integer – any positive or negative whole number or zero, for example, -2, -1, 0, 1, 2 ...

Factor – a natural number which divides exactly into another number (no remainder), for example, the factors of 12 are 1, 2, 3, 4, 6 and 12

Multiple – the multiples of a number are the products of its multiplication table, for example, the multiples of 3 are 3, 6, 9, 12, 15 ...

Least common multiple (LCM) – the lowest multiple which is common to two or more numbers, for example,

the multiples of 3 are 3, 6, 9, 12, 15, 18, 24, 27, 30, 33, 36 ...

the multiples of 4 are 4, 8, 12, 16, 20, 24, 28, 32, 36 ...

the common multiples are 12, 24, 36 ...

the least common multiple is 12

Common factor – factors that are in common for two or more numbers, for example,

the factors of 6 are 1, 2, 3, 6

the factors of 9 are 1, 3, 9

the common factors are 1 and 3

Highest common factor (HCF) – the highest factor that two or more numbers have in common, for example,

the factors of 16 are 1, 2, 4, 8, 16

the factors of 24 are 1, 2, 3, 4, 6, 8, 12, 24

the common factors are 1, 2, 4, 8

the highest common factor is 8

Prime number – a natural number with exactly two factors, for example, 2 (factors are 1 and 2), 3 (factors are 1 and 3), 5 (factors are 1 and 5), 7, 11, 13, 17, 23, ... 59 ...

Index notation – when a product such as $2 \times 2 \times 2 \times 2$ is written as 2^4, the 4 is the index (plural **indices**)

Prime factor decomposition – writing a number as the product of its prime factors, for example, $12 = 2^2 \times 3$

Reciprocal – any number multiplied by its reciprocal equals one; one divided by a number will give its reciprocal, for example, the reciprocal of 3 is $\frac{1}{3}$ because $3 \times \frac{1}{3} = 1$

Learn 1   Factors and multiples

Examples:

a What are the factors of 28?

1   2   4   7   14   28

In most cases factors are in pairs
$1 \times 28 = 28$
$2 \times 14 = 28$
$4 \times 7 = 28$

b What are the first five multiples of 4?

4   8   12   16   20

All of the numbers are in the four times table

c What is the least common multiple (LCM) of 6 and 8?

6   12   18   24   30 ———— These numbers are all multiples of 6

8   16   24   32   40 ———— These numbers are all multiples of 8

The LCM of 6 and 8 is 24.

24 is the smallest number that is common to both lists

d What is the highest common factor (HCF) of 16 and 24?

1   2   4   8   16 ———— These numbers are all factors of 16

1   2   3   4   6   8   12   24 ———— These numbers are all factors of 24

1   2   4   8 ———— 1, 2, 4, 8 are common factors of 16 and 24

The HCF of 16 and 24 is 8.

8 is the highest number that is common to both lists

Apply 1

1 Write down all the factors of:

  a 15   **d** 10   **g** 32

  b 64   **e** 40   **h** 72

  c 48   **f** 36   **i** 84

2 Write down the first five multiples of:

  a 2   **d** 6   **g** 11

  b 5   **e** 9   **h** 8

  c 7   **f** 12   **i** 13

3 Find the LCM of these sets of numbers.

a 6 and 15   **d** 3 and 8   **g** 3, 5 and 6

b 12 and 6   **e** 4 and 6   <u>**h**</u> 6, 8 and 32

c 5 and 7   **f** 4, 10 and 12

4 What are the common factors of:

a 6 and 15   **c** 4 and 64   **e** 25 and 40

b 9 and 48   **d** 10 and 16   **f** 24 and 36?

5 Find the HCF of these pairs of numbers.

a 6 and 15   **d** 24 and 36   **g** 27 and 36

b 12 and 15   <u>**e**</u> 56 and 152

c 32 and 48   **f** 84 and 70

6 The HCF of two numbers is 5. Give five possible pairs of numbers.

7 Write down all the factors of 20 and 24. Hence find the common factors and write down the HCF of 20 and 24.

8 Get Real!

A lighthouse flashes every 56 seconds. Another lighthouse flashes every 40 seconds. At 9 p.m. they both flash at the same time. What time will it be when they next both flash at the same time?

9 Get Real!

Alison is making her own birthday cards. She needs to cut up lengths of ribbon. Find the smallest length of ribbon that can be cut into an exact number of either 5 cm or 8 cm or 12 cm lengths.

10 Get Real!

One political party holds its annual conference at Eastbourne every four years. Another holds its annual conference there every six years. They both held their conference in Eastbourne in 2006. When will they next be there in the same year?

11 Get Real!

Nick visits his grandparents every two days. Briony visits them every three days. If they both visit on a Monday, on which day do they next both visit?

12 Richard always goes to his local café on a Saturday afternoon. Zoë works there on every third afternoon. She serves Richard one Saturday afternoon. How many weeks will it be before she will serve him again?

<u>**13**</u> A farmer has 24 cows and 30 sheep. She decides to divide these equally between her sons.

a What is the greatest number of sons she could have?

She increases her livestock to 40 cows and 72 sheep.

b What is the greatest number of sons she could now have?

14 Emily sets her alarm clock using the town hall clock. The problem is that the town hall clock gains one hour a day. How long will it be until both clocks next show the same time?

Explore

◎ Write down all the numbers between 1 and 30

◎ Work out the number of factors for each number

◎ Can you work out a rule for numbers that have:

a two factors only

b an odd number of factors?

> **Investigate further**

Explore

◎ The factors of 6 are 1, 2, 3 and 6. If you ignore the 6 then the other factors add up to make 6

◎ 6 is a **perfect number** because $1 + 2 + 3 = 6$

◎ A number whose factors (not including itself) sum to more than itself is called an **abundant number**

◎ A number whose factors (not including itself) sum to less than itself is called a **deficient number**

> **Investigate further**

Learn 2   Prime numbers and prime factor decomposition

Example: Find the prime factors of 40.

Start by finding the smallest prime number that divides into 40.
Continue dividing by successive prime numbers until the answer becomes 1.

2	40
2	20
2	10
5	5
	1

Prime numbers are numbers with exactly two factors, for example, 2, 3, 5, 7, 11, 13, ...

The prime factors of 40 are 2, 2, 2, 5.
40 written as a product of prime factors is $2 \times 2 \times 2 \times 5$.
This can be written as $2^3 \times 5$.

This is called 'index notation'. The index tells you how many times the factor 2 occurs

Apply 2

1 Sam describes a number in the following way:
'It is a prime number. It is a factor of 21. It is not a factor of 12.'
What number is she describing?

2 Chris describes a number in the following way:
'It is below 100. It is a multiple of 6. It is also a multiple of 4.
The sum of its digits is a prime number.'
What number is he describing?

3 Make up two number descriptions of your own.

4 Write each of the following numbers as a product of prime factors.

a 20   c 36   e 90   g 63   i 84
b 18   d 66   f 100   h 48   j 96

5 Express each number as a product of its prime factors.

a 24   b 72   c 45

6 Express each number as a product of its prime factors.
Write your answers using index notation.

a 220   c 136   e 720   g 390   i 624
b 144   d 300   f 480   h 450   j 216

7 Clare says that one must be a prime number. Is she correct? Explain your answer.

<u>8</u> Write 2420 as a product of its prime factors. Write your answer using index notation.

<u>9</u> Write 9240 as a product of its prime factors. Write your answer using index notation.

<u>10</u> Write 8820 as a product of its prime factors. Write your answer using index notation.

<u>11</u> If $1080 = 2^x \times 3^y \times 5^z$, what are the values of x, y and z?

Explore

You will need a 100 square
◎ Cross out the number 1
◎ Put a circle round the number 2 and then cross out all of the other multiples of 2
◎ Put a circle round the next number after 2 that has not been crossed out
◎ Cross out all of the other multiples of that number
◎ Put a circle round the next number not crossed out and cross out every multiple of that number
◎ Continue until you run out of numbers in the 100 square

What do you notice about the numbers that are left?

Investigate further

Learn 3   Reciprocals

Examples: Find the reciprocal of: **a** 5   **b** $\frac{1}{4}$ **c** 0.3   **d** $2\frac{1}{2}$

You can write 5 as $\frac{5}{1}$

The reciprocal of $\frac{5}{1}$ is $\frac{1}{5}$

a The reciprocal of 5 is $\frac{1}{5}$

b The reciprocal of $\frac{1}{4}$ is $\frac{4}{1} = 4$ ⟵——— It is better to write $\frac{4}{1}$ as 4

c The reciprocal of 0.3 is the same as ⟵——— Write 0.3 as a fraction
the reciprocal of $\frac{3}{10}$

The reciprocal of $\frac{3}{10}$ is $\frac{10}{3} = 3\frac{1}{3}$ ⟵——— It is better to write $\frac{10}{3}$ as $3\frac{1}{3}$

d The reciprocal of $2\frac{1}{2}$ is the same as ⟵——— Write $2\frac{1}{2}$ as $\frac{5}{2}$
the reciprocal of $\frac{5}{2}$

The reciprocal of $\frac{5}{2}$ is $\frac{2}{5}$

The reciprocal of 0 is not defined and your calculator
will give an error for $\frac{1}{0}$

Apply 3

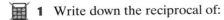

1 Write down the reciprocal of:

   a 4   **b** 6   **c** 8   **d** 10   **e** 7   **f** 0.25

2 Find the reciprocal of:

   a $\frac{1}{2}$ **b** $\frac{1}{5}$ **c** $\frac{1}{7}$ **d** $\frac{1}{8}$ **e** $\frac{1}{12}$ **f** 0.8

3 Find the reciprocal of:

   a $\frac{2}{7}$ **b** $\frac{3}{5}$ **c** $\frac{2}{3}$ **d** $\frac{5}{6}$ **e** $\frac{3}{11}$

4 Write down the reciprocal of:

   a 0.3   **b** 0.7   **c** 0.4   **d** 0.125   **e** $0.\dot{3}$

5 Find the reciprocal of:

   a $2\frac{1}{4}$ **b** $3\frac{1}{2}$ **c** $1\frac{3}{4}$ **d** 1.25   **e** 3.6   **f** $1.\dot{6}$

<u>6</u> Find the reciprocals of the numbers 2 to 12, as decimals. If they are not exact,
write them as recurring decimals. Which of the numbers have reciprocals that:

   a are exact decimals

   b have one recurring figure

   c have two recurring figures?

Explore

◎ Write down the reciprocals of $2, 1, \frac{1}{2}, \frac{1}{4}, \frac{1}{8} \ldots$

◎ Continue the pattern

◎ What do you notice?

Investigate further

Integers

ASSESS

The following exercise tests your understanding of this chapter, with the questions appearing in order of increasing difficulty.

1 At a party it was discovered that Siobhan, Gareth, Nathan and Ulrika had birthdays on the 6th, 15th, 27th and 30th of the month.
Sven joined the group and it was discovered that his birthday was a factor of everyone else's.
If Sven was not born on the 1st, on what day of the month was Sven born?

2 Find the prime factors of:

  a 420

  b 13 475

3 Amrit says that the value of the expression $n^2 + n + 41$, where $n = 0, 1, 2, 3, \ldots$ always gives prime numbers.

  a Show this is true for $n = 0$ to 5.

  b Without any calculation, name one value of n that disproves Amrit's theory.

4 Find the reciprocals of:

  a 5

  b -8

  c $\frac{5}{8}$

  d -0.2

  e $0.\dot{2}$

5 a What is the only number that is the same as its reciprocal?

  b What is the only number that has no reciprocal?
  Explain your answer.

6 Sam says he knows a different way of finding the HCF of two numbers. He says:

1 Write down the numbers side by side.
2 Cross out the largest number and write underneath it the difference between the two numbers.
3 Repeat step 2 until the two numbers left are the same.
4 The remaining number is the HCF of the two original numbers.

Try Sam's method with the following numbers:

a 16 and 36

b 60 and 225

c 456 and 640

d Does the method work with three numbers? Investigate.

Try some real past exam questions to test your knowledge:

7 Tom, Sam and Matt are counting drum beats.

Tom hits a snare drum every 2 beats.
Sam hits a kettle drum every 5 beats.
Matt hits a bass drum every 8 beats.

Tom, Sam and Matt start by hitting their drums at the same time.
How many beats is it before Tom, Sam and Matt **next** hit their drums at the **same** time?

Spec A, Higher Paper 1, June 04

8 a Express 144 as the product of its prime factors.
Write your answer in index form.

b Find the highest common factor (HCF) of 60 and 144.

Spec B, Mod 3 Intermediate, June 03

D **Examiners would normally expect students who get a D grade to be able to:**

Estimate answers to calculations such as $\dfrac{22.6 \times 18.7}{5.2}$

C **Examiners would normally expect students who get a C grade also to be able to:**

Estimate answers to calculations such as $\dfrac{22.6 \times 18.7}{0.52}$

Find minimum and maximum values

B **Examiners would normally expect students who get a B grade also to be able to:**

Round to a given number of significant figures

What you should already know ...

- Round numbers to the nearest 1000, nearest 100, nearest 10, nearest integer, significant figures, decimal places ...

- Estimate calculations involving decimals
- Estimate square roots

Round – give an approximate value of a number. Numbers can be rounded to the nearest 1000, nearest 100, nearest 10, nearest integer, significant figures, decimal places ... etc

Significant figures – the digits in a number; the closer a digit is to the beginning of a number then the more important or significant it is; for example, in the number 23.657, 2 is the most significant digit and is worth 20, 7 is the least significant digit and is worth $\frac{7}{1000}$; the number 23.657 has 5 significant digits

Decimal places – the digits to the right of a decimal point in a number, for example, in the number 23.657, the number 6 is the first decimal place (worth $\frac{6}{10}$), the number 5 is the second decimal place (worth $\frac{5}{100}$) and 7 is the third decimal place (worth $\frac{7}{1000}$); the number 23.657 has 3 decimal places

Upper bound – this is the maximum possible value of a measurement, for example, if a length is measured as 37 cm correct to the nearest centimetre, the upper bound of the length is 37.5 cm

Lower bound – this is the minimum possible value of a measurement, for example, if a length is measured as 37 cm correct to the nearest centimetre, the lower bound of the length is 36.5 cm

Degree of accuracy – the accuracy to which a measurement or a number is given, for example, to the nearest 1000, nearest 100, nearest 10, nearest integer, 2 significant figures, 3 decimal places

Estimate – find an approximate value of a calculation; this is usually found by rounding all of the numbers to one significant figure, for example, $\dfrac{20.4 \times 4.3}{5.2}$ is approximately $\dfrac{20 \times 4}{5}$ where each number is rounded to 1 s.f.; the answer can be worked out in your head to give 16

Learn 1　Estimating

Example:　Estimate the answer to 3.86×2.14

Round all the numbers to one significant figure, then work out the approximate answer in your head.

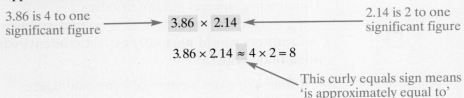

3.86 is 4 to one significant figure → 3.86×2.14 ← 2.14 is 2 to one significant figure

$$3.86 \times 2.14 \approx 4 \times 2 = 8$$

This curly equals sign means 'is approximately equal to'

It is easy to make mistakes when using decimals, so it is a good idea to estimate to find the approximate size of the answer so that you can see if you are right.

Apply 1

1　For each question, decide which is the best estimate.

		Estimate A	Estimate B	Estimate C
a	2.89×9.4	2.7	18	27
b	1.2×29.4	3	30	300
c	$9.17 \div 3.2$	3	4	18
d	48.5×9.8	5	50	500
e	$4.2 \div 1.9$	1	2	3
f	22.4×6.1	12	120	180
g	$7.8 \div 1.2$	8	78	80
h	$2.1 \times 3.1 \div 4.2$	1	1.5	2
i	$20.9 \div 6.9 \times 4.1$	10	11	12

2 Estimate the answers to these calculations by rounding to one significant figure. You may wish to use a calculator to check your answers.

a $2.9 + 3.2$

f $4.3 - 3.7$

k $\dfrac{102.4 + 8.7}{0.22}$

b $7.9 \div 2.2$

g 5.3×8.2

l $\dfrac{102.4 \times 8.7}{0.22}$

c $67.8 + 22.1$

h $\dfrac{20.4 \times 7.7}{0.52}$

m $21.3(7.56 + 3.89)$

d $\dfrac{20.4 \times 7.7}{5.2}$

i $\dfrac{75.5 \times 2.7}{0.12}$

n $21.3(7.56 - 3.89)$

e 0.2×5.4

j $\dfrac{28.5 + 53}{64.1 - 53.7}$

> **HINT** Be careful when dividing by numbers less than one.

3 For each pair of calculations, estimate the answers to help decide which will have the bigger answer.
Use a calculator to check your answers

a 5.2×1.8 or 3.1×2.95

c $9.723 + 4.28$ or $39.4 \div 2.04$

b $28.4 \div 5.9$ or 2.03×3.78

d 39.5×21.3 or 81.3×7.8

4 The square root of 10 lies between the square root of 9 and the square root of 16. The square root of 9 is 3 and the square root of 16 is 4, so the answer lies between 3 and 4.

Use this method to estimate the square root of:

a 12   **b** 20   **c** 50   **d** 3   **e** 1000

5 Estimate 5.92×3.82 by rounding to the nearest whole number.
Explain why the answer is an over-estimate of the exact answer.

6 Sam says, 'I estimated the answer to $16.7 - 8.6$ as 8 by rounding up both numbers, so the answer is an over-estimate.' Show that Sam is not correct.

7 Ali says, '35 divided by 5 is 7, so 35 divided by 0.5 is 0.7'.
Is Ali right? Give a reason for your answer.

8 Give one example that shows that dividing can make something smaller and another to show that dividing can make something bigger.

9 Hannah says:

- When I rounded the numbers in a calculation I got $\dfrac{110}{0.2}$

- Then I multiplied the top and the bottom both by 10 to give $\dfrac{1100}{2}$

- So the answer is 550.

Is Hannah correct? Give a reason for your answer.

10 a Find five numbers whose square roots are between 7 and 8.

b Find two consecutive whole numbers to complete this statement:
'The square root of 60 is between ... and ... '

11 Get Real!

Estimate the total cost of three books costing £3.99, £5.25 and £10.80

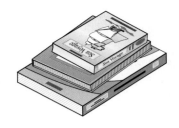

12 Get Real!

Estimate the length of fencing needed for this field.

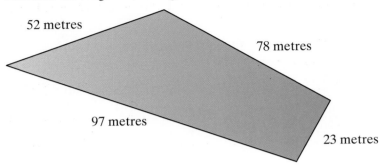

52 metres

78 metres

97 metres

23 metres

13 Get Real!

Anne's car goes 6.2 miles on every litre of petrol. Estimate how far she can drive if her fuel tank has 24.5 litres in it.

14 Get Real!

A group of 18 people wins £389 540 on the lottery. Estimate how much each person will get when the money is shared out equally.

Pay: _____ 20 __
The sum of: _____ £ 389 540

15 Get Real!

It's Harry's birthday! He asks his mum for a cake like a football pitch. She makes a cake that is 29 cm wide and 38 cm long.

a She wants to put a ribbon round the cake. She can buy ribbon in various lengths: 1 m, 1.5 m, 2 m, 2.5 m or 3 m.
Estimate the perimeter of the cake and say which length ribbon she should buy.

b She can buy ready-made green icing for the top of the cake. The icing comes in packs to cover 1000 cm². Estimate the area of the top of the cake and decide whether one pack will be enough.

Explore

◎ You know that $20 \times 30 = 600$
So the answers to all these calculations will be close to 600, as the numbers are close to 20×30:

a 19.4×28.7 **c** 18.8×29.6 **e** 29.8×20.4 **g** 23.4×33.4
b 23.4×30.2 **d** 21.2×30.4 **f** 31.4×18.7 **h** 22.3×29.8

◎ Can you decide which answers will be less than 600, and which will be more than 600?

◎ Check your predictions with a calculator

◎ When can you be sure an estimate is lower than the actual answer?

◎ When can you be sure an estimate is higher than the actual answer?

Investigate further

Explore

◎ You know that 8 ÷ 2 = 4
Use a calculator to divide numbers close to 8 by numbers close to 2
For example, you might try 8.2 ÷ 1.9 and 7.8 ÷ 1.8

◎ Can you decide which answers will be less than 4, and which will be more than 4?

◎ Check your predictions with a calculator

◎ When can you be sure an estimate is lower than the actual answer?

◎ When can you be sure an estimate is higher than the actual answer?

Investigate further

Learn 2   Finding minimum and maximum values

Example:

The length of a table is measured as 60 cm, correct to the nearest centimetre. What are the minimum and maximum possible lengths of the table?

All these numbers are nearer to 60 than they are to 59 or to 61

60.5 rounds up to 61

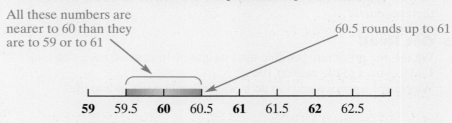

| 59 | 59.5 | 60 | 60.5 | 61 | 61.5 | 62 | 62.5 |

Any length given to the nearest centimetre could be up to half a centimetre smaller or larger than the given value.

A length given to the nearest centimetre as 60 cm could be anything between 59.5 cm and 60.5 cm. The minimum and maximum possible lengths are 59.5 cm and 60.5 cm or $59.5 \leqslant x < 60.5$

The length cannot actually be 60.5 cm, as this measurement rounds up to 61 cm – but it can be as close to 60.5 cm as you like, so 60.5 cm is the top limit (or **upper bound**) of the length

Apply 2

1   Each of these quantities is rounded to the nearest whole number of units.
    Write down the minimum and maximum possible size of each quantity.

    a 54 cm

    b 5 kg

    c 26 m

    d 17 ml

    e £45

    f 175 g

2 Jane says,
'If a length is 78 cm to the nearest centimetre, then
the maximum possible length is 78.49 cm.'
Is Jane right? Explain your answer.

3 The volume of water in a tank is given as 1500 litres.

a Decide if the volume has been rounded to the nearest litre,
nearest 10 litres or nearest 100 litres if the minimum possible volume is

i 1450 ℓ **ii** 1499.5 ℓ **iii** 1495 ℓ

b If the actual volume is V litres, complete this statement in each case: ... $\leqslant V <$ ....

c Explain why there is a 'less than or equal to' sign before the V but a
'less than' sign after the V.

d How do you know that a volume written as 1500 litres has not been
measured to the nearest tenth of a litre?

4 Get Real!
ChocoBars should weigh 40 grams with a tolerance of 5% either way.
If the bars weigh 40 grams correct to the nearest 10 grams, will they be
within the tolerance? Show how you worked out your answer.
Why do you think that manufacturers have a 'tolerance' in the sizes of
their products?

5 Get Real!
What is the maximum possible total weight of 10 cartons, each weighing
1.4 kg correct to the nearest 100 g?
Why might someone need to do a calculation like this in real life?

Explore

- ◎ Write a note to explain to someone else how to find the maximum and
minimum possible ages of a person whose age is given as a whole number
of years, for example, 8 years

- ◎ Write a note to explain to someone else how to find the maximum and
minimum possible amounts of money when the quantity is given to the
nearest pound, for example £18

Investigate further

Rounding

The following exercise tests your understanding of this chapter, with the questions appearing in order of increasing difficulty.

1 The average person's heart beats about once a second. Estimate how many times it beats during a year.

2 The (movement) energy of an athlete of mass 43 kg running at a velocity of 9.7 m/s can be found by working out $43 \times 9.7 \times 9.7 \div 2$. Use appropriate approximations for 43 and 9.7 and estimate the athlete's energy.

3 Ngugi lives on the equator, which is a circle of diameter 12 756 km. George lives in the UK on a circle of latitude with diameter 7854 km. To calculate the distance each boy moves in one day due to the Earth's rotation we multiply each diameter by 3.14

Write all three values given above correct to **the nearest thousand** and hence estimate how much further Ngugi travels than George in one day.

4 Estimate the value of   a $\dfrac{24.8 \times 3.2}{0.54}$ b $\dfrac{29.9 + \sqrt{0.918}}{(16.2 - 6.15)^2}$

5 a The length of a rectangle is given as 27 m correct to the nearest m. Write down the minimum and maximum possible lengths it could be.

   b A different length is given as 5.0 cm correct to nearest mm. Write down the minimum and maximum possible lengths it could be.

6 Copy and complete the table below.

Starting number	To two significant figures	To three significant figures	To one decimal place	To two decimal places
186.487		186		
3.14159	3.1			
0.51627			0.5	
0.0080990				
8				

7 Estimate the value of $25 \times 4.2 + \dfrac{5(93.1 - 32 \times 2.4)}{11.3 + 9.1}$

Try some real past exam questions to test your knowledge:

8 a Work out 600×0.3

   b Work out $600 \div 0.3$

   c You are told that $432 \times 21 = 9072$
   Write down the value of $9072 \div 2.1$

   d Find an approximate value of $\dfrac{2987}{21 \times 49}$
   You **must** show all your working.

Spec A, Int Paper 1, Nov 03

9 This is a true statement.

I am 18 years old.

Write down:

a the minimum age that Kylie could be

b the maximum age that Kylie could be.

Spec B, Int Paper 1, Mar 04

3 Decimals

D **Examiners would normally expect students who get a D grade to be able to:**

Multiply two decimals such as 2.4×0.7

Convert decimals to fractions and fractions to decimals

C **Examiners would normally expect students who get a C grade also to be able to:**

Divide a number by a decimal such as $1 \div 0.2$ and $2.8 \div 0.07$

B **Examiners would normally expect students who get a B grade also to be able to:**

Identify recurring and terminating decimals

Convert recurring decimals to fractions and fractions to recurring decimals

What you should already know ...

- Add, subtract, multiply and divide whole numbers
- Add and subtract decimals
- Estimate answers to questions involving decimals

Digit – any of the numerals from 0 to 9

Decimal – a number in which a decimal point separates the whole number part from the decimal part, for example, 24.8

Numerator – the number on the top of a fraction

Numerator ⟶ $\dfrac{3}{8}$ ⟵ Denominator

Denominator – the number on the bottom of a fraction

Terminating decimal – a decimal that ends, for example, 0.3, 0.33 or 0.3333

Recurring decimal – a decimal with a repeating digit or group of digits, for example, 0.33333333333 ... (written as $0.\dot{3}$) or 0.25678678678678 ... (written as $0.25\dot{6}7\dot{8}$)

Learn 1 Multiplying decimals

Example: Calculate 0.78×5.2

First remove decimal points: 78×52

Then multiply in your usual way
(The grid method is shown here,
but use your usual method.)

×	**70**	**8**
50	3500	400
2	140	16

$$\begin{array}{r} 3500 \\ 400 \\ 140 \\ +\quad 16 \\ \hline 4056 \end{array}$$

Finally, put the decimal point back in the answer.

Estimate that 0.78×5.2 is about $1 \times 5 = 5$.

So $0.78 \times 5.2 = 4.056$

Alternatively, count up the number of decimal places in the question.

There are three decimal places in the question: 0.78×5.2

So you need three decimal places in the answer: 4.056

So $0.78 \times 5.2 = 4.056$

Apply 1

1 Use the multiplication $23 \times 52 = 1196$ to help you to complete the questions.

   a 2.3×52 **d** 0.23×52 **g** $0.023 \times 520\,000$

   b 2.3×520 **e** 0.23×0.52

   c 0.23×5.2 **f** $23\,000 \times 0.052$

2 Calculate:

   a 0.13×22 **e** 1.7×0.22 **i** 8.7×2.51

   b 1.5×2.3 **f** 3.2×13 **j** 8.93×162

   c 0.7×1.3 **g** 5.1×2.3 **k** $73.1 \times 12\,400$

   d 1.1×4.5 **h** 2.7×0.13 **l** $14.3 \times 223\,000$

3 Using your answers to question **2**, write down the answers to these.

   a 1.3×22 **e** 17×2.2 **i** 0.087×0.0251

   b 1.5×0.23 **f** 0.032×13 **j** 0.00893×0.0162

   c 0.07×1.3 **g** 0.0051×0.23 **k** 7.31×1.24

   d 0.11×0.45 **h** 27×1.3 **l** 1430×22.3

4 A can of Fizzicola contains 0.3 litres of drink. A box holds 36 cans.
How many litres of Fizzicola are there in a box?

5 Here are two multiplagons. On each straight line, the numbers in the circles multiply together to make the number in the rectangle.

Your job is to copy and complete the multiplagons by filling in the missing numbers.

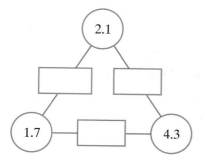 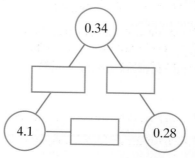

6 Get Real!

Rachel is making some curtains. She buys 4.2 metres of fabric. The fabric costs £3.85 per metre.

a How much does Rachel have to pay?

b The fabric is 1.2 metres wide. What area of fabric has Rachel bought?

7 $87 \times 132 = 11\ 484$.

Use this fact to write down the answers to these multiplications.

a 8.7×1.32

b 87×0.132

c 0.87×13.2

d $870 \times 13\ 200$

e 1.32×870

f $114.84 \div 132$

g $11.484 \div 8.7$

8 Toby says $0.4 \times 0.2 = 0.8$
Austin says it isn't, because $4 \times 0.2 = 0.8$
Austin says $0.4 \times 0.2 = 0.08$
Toby says it isn't because that's less than you started with.
Who is right, Toby or Austin? Give a reason for your answer.

9 a You know $3 \times 2 = 6$.
So what is 0.3×0.2?

b What other multiplications have the same answer as 0.3×0.2?

c Write down five multiplications with an answer of 0.12

10 Work out the area of this shape.

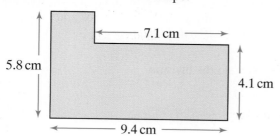

11 Think of a number.
Write it down.
Divide it by 2.
Divide the answer by 2.
Write down your answer.

Go back to your starting number.
Multiply it by 0.25
Write down your answer.
Can you explain why your answers are the same?

Explore

◎ Add together 1.125 and 9

◎ Now multiply 1.125 by 9

◎ You should get the same answer to both questions

Can you find other pairs of numbers with this characteristic?

Can you find a pair where the product is twice the sum?

(Investigate further)

Learn 2 Dividing decimals

Examples:

a Calculate $31.2 \div 0.4$

$31.2 \div 0.4 = \frac{31.2}{0.4}$

$= \frac{31.2}{0.4} = \frac{312}{4}$ — Make the fraction an equivalent fraction by multiplying the numerator and denominator by 10

$\begin{array}{r} 78 \\ 4\overline{)312} \end{array}$ ← — Now do the division

So $31.2 \div 0.4 = 78$

b Calculate $3.8 \div 0.05$

$3.8 \div 0.05 = \frac{3.8}{0.05}$

$= \frac{3.8}{0.05} = \frac{38}{0.5} = \frac{380}{5}$ — Make the fraction an equivalent fraction by multiplying the numerator and denominator by 10 and 10 again

$\begin{array}{r} 76 \\ 5\overline{)380} \end{array}$ ← — Now do the division

So $3.8 \div 0.05 = 76$

Apply 2

1 Write these calculations as equivalent fractions and work them out.

   a $3.2 \div 0.4$ **e** $53.1 \div 0.3$ **i** $0.056 \div 0.7$

   b $25.4 \div 0.2$ **f** $1.74 \div 0.6$ **j** $13.2 \div 400$

   c $2.85 \div 0.5$ **g** $0.4 \div 0.08$ **k** $0.028 \div 700$

   d $42.2 \div 0.02$ **h** $32 \div 0.8$

2 Write these calculations as equivalent fractions and work them out.

   a $4.07 \div 1.1$ **f** $25.3 \div 0.11$ **k** $222.89 \div 3.1$

   b $22.8 \div 1.2$ **g** $7.392 \div 0.11$ **l** $83.16 \div 2200$

   c $2.73 \div 0.13$ **h** $0.474 \div 0.12$ **m** $12.45 \div 15\,000$

   d $0.264 \div 1.1$ **i** $0.0552 \div 0.012$ **n** $56.2 \div 250$

   e $16.8 \div 0.12$ **j** $0.945 \div 1.4$

3 Get Real!

Malcolm the plumber has a 6 metre length of copper pipe.
He needs to cut it into 0.4 metre lengths.
How many pieces will he get?

4 Get Real!

On her birthday, Bridget is given a big box of small sweets
called Little Diamonds.
She wants to find out how many sweets are in the box, but it
would take too long to count them.
A label on the box tells her that the total weight is 500 g.
She weighs 10 sweets. The weight of the 10 sweets is 0.4 g.

   a How much does one sweet weigh?

   b How many sweets are there in the box?

5 Hazel says that $48 \div 2 = 24$, so $48 \div 0.2 = 2.4$
Darren says $48 \div 2 = 24$, so $4.8 \div 0.2 = 2.4$
Harry says $48 \div 2 = 24$, so $4.8 \div 2 = 2.4$
Who is right? Give a reason for your answer.

<u>6</u> €1 is worth £0.60. How many euro would you get for £7.50?

<u>7</u> Here are two multiplagons.
On each straight line, the numbers in the circles multiply
together to make the number in the rectangle.
Your job is to copy and complete them by filling in the missing numbers.

  a   **b**

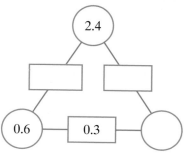
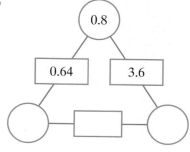

8 Carrie knows that $3.4 \div 0.4 = 8.5$
Use this to copy and fill in the gaps in these questions.

a $34 \div 0.4 = \boxed{}$

c $340 \div \boxed{} = 8.5$

e $\boxed{} \div 0.04 = 8.5$

b $3.4 \div 4 = \boxed{}$

d $\boxed{} \div 4 = 0.85$

f $0.34 \div 8.5 = \boxed{}$

9 Start with a number less than 1.
Take it away from 1.
Divide the first number by the second.
Divide this number by one more than itself.
You end up with the starting number!

Example:

$$0.8$$
$$1 - 0.8 = 0.2$$
$$0.8 \div 0.2 = 8 \div 2 = 4$$
$$4 \div 5 = 0.8$$

Try this yourself, starting with

a 0.5   **b** 0.9   **c** 0.75

Check it with any number you like – although you will probably need a calculator for more difficult examples.

10 Use $43 \times 28 = 1204$ to write down the answers to these divisions.

a $1204 \div 43$

d $120.4 \div 2.8$

g $1.204 \div 430$

b $12.04 \div 43$

e $120\,400 \div 0.43$

h $12.04 \div 8.6$

c $1.204 \div 2.8$

f $0.1204 \div 280$

Explore

◎ Draw a grid like this one:

◎ Roll a dice

◎ Write the score in one of the empty boxes in your grid

◎ Roll the dice twice more, writing the score in a box after each roll

◎ Work out the answer to the division

◎ Now try again – your aim is to get the highest possible answer

> Investigate further

Learn 3   Fractions and decimals

Examples: **a** Write 0.72 as a fraction.

To change a decimal to a fraction, just remember the place values.

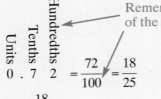

Remember to use the place value of the *last* digit as the denominator

$$0\,.\,7\,2 = \frac{72}{100} = \frac{18}{25}$$

The numerator and denominator have been divided by 4

$$0.72 = \frac{18}{25}$$

b Write $\frac{7}{8}$ as a decimal.

$\frac{7}{8}$ means $7 \div 8$.

$$\begin{array}{r} 0\,.\,8\,7\,5 \\ 8\overline{\smash{)}7\,.\,{}^7 0\,{}^6 0\,{}^4 0} \end{array}$$

You can check your answers with a calculator

$\frac{7}{8} = 0.875$

Apply 3

1 Write these decimals as fractions, giving your answers in their simplest form:

a 0.6   **b** 0.32   **c** 0.125   **d** 0.995

2 a Write these fractions as decimals.

i $\frac{2}{5}$ **ii** $\frac{3}{8}$ **iii** $\frac{7}{20}$

b Use your answers to part **a** to write the fractions in order of size, starting with the smallest.

3 Which of these fractions is closest to 0.67?

a $\frac{3}{4}$ **b** $\frac{5}{8}$ **c** $\frac{3}{5}$ **d** $\frac{13}{20}$

> HINT
> 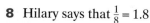 Write the fractions as decimals.

4 a What is 2.65 as a fraction?

b What is $3\frac{7}{20}$ as a decimal?

5 Write down five fractions that are equal to 0.4

6 Get Real!
At a school fête, some children decided to raise money with a 'Guess the weight of the cake' stall.
Amy guessed 3300 g, Tariq guessed 3.28 kg and Caroline guessed $3\frac{1}{5}$ kg.
The real weight was 3.237 kg. Who won?

7 Josh divided one number by another, and 2.375 was the answer. Both numbers were less than 20. What were the two numbers?

8 Hilary says that $\frac{1}{8} = 1.8$
Nick says $\frac{3}{8} = 0.38$
Eleanor says $\frac{1}{10} = 0.10$
Jeff says $\frac{1}{20} = 0.20$
Who is correct? Correct the errors of the others.

9 Dan knows that $\frac{1}{8} = 0.125$
Use this answer to change these fractions to decimals.

a $\frac{3}{8}$ **b** $1\frac{1}{8}$ **c** $\frac{5}{8}$ **d** $\frac{1}{16}$

10 Write these fractions as decimals. Be careful – they never end! They are called recurring decimals. Stop when you have reached a repeating digit or pattern of digits.

    a $\frac{2}{3}$ **b** $\frac{4}{11}$ **c** $\frac{3}{7}$

11 Find three fractions that fit all these rules:

    a All three fractions must have different denominators.

    b Each denominator must be less than 10.

    c The fraction must be greater than 0.2

    d The fraction must be less than 0.3

12 Use a calculator to change these fractions to decimals.

    a $\frac{3}{16}$ **b** $\frac{7}{32}$ **c** $\frac{5}{80}$ **d** $\frac{17}{8}$ **e** $2\frac{11}{40}$ **f** $3\frac{9}{64}$

Explore

  ◎ Change all the unit fractions ($\frac{1}{2}, \frac{1}{3}, \frac{1}{4}, \frac{1}{5}, ...$) up to $\frac{1}{10}$ to decimals

  ◎ Which give recurring decimals and which give terminating decimals?

          Investigate further

Learn 4   Recurring decimals and fractions

Example: Write $\frac{7}{11}$ as a decimal.

$\frac{7}{11}$ means $7 \div 11$.

$$11\overline{)7.^70^40^70^40\,...}$$
$$\qquad 0.\,6\ 3\ 6\ 3\,...$$

You can check your answers with a calculator

The recurring decimal 0.6363636363 ... is written as $0.\dot{6}\dot{3}$

Similarly:
The recurring decimal 0.3333333333 ... is written as $0.\dot{3}$
The recurring decimal 0.54789789789 ... is written as $0.54\dot{7}8\dot{9}$

Apply 4

1 Which of these fractions will give recurring decimals?

a $\frac{4}{15}$ **d** $\frac{5}{6}$ **g** $\frac{9}{60}$

b $\frac{7}{18}$ **e** $\frac{3}{20}$ **h** $\frac{13}{125}$

c $\frac{5}{16}$ **f** $\frac{5}{9}$

2 Write these fractions as recurring decimals.

a $\frac{2}{3}$ **b** $\frac{7}{11}$ **c** $\frac{4}{7}$ **d** $\frac{5}{13}$

3 **Get Real!**

According to the rules of football, the circumference of the ball must be between 68 cm and 70 cm.

To make it easier to check, a club chairman makes up a frame as shown. He says that a ball with a circumference of 69 cm will just fit inside the frame.

a Divide the circumference of 69 cm by the diameter, 22 cm.

b Explain why this answer is about the right size.

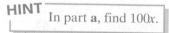
← 22 cm →

4 Suppose we want to change $0.\dot{1}6\dot{2}$ to a fraction.
Follow the reasoning below.

Suppose $x = 0.\dot{1}6\dot{2}$ (A)
Then $1000x = 162.\dot{1}6\dot{2}$ (B)
Subtracting (B) – (A): $999x = 162$
$$x = \frac{162}{999} = \frac{18}{111} = \frac{6}{37}$$

Use the same approach to turn these recurring decimals into fractions in their smallest form.

a $0.\dot{1}\dot{8}$ **b** $0.4\dot{2}\dot{3}$ **c** $0.\dot{1}38\dot{6}$

> **HINT**
> In part **a**, find $100x$.

5 Can you write a simple rule for changing any recurring decimal to a fraction?

6 Charlotte knows that $\frac{4}{11} = 0.\dot{3}\dot{6}$, but she mistakenly writes it as $0.3\dot{6}$
Write $0.3\dot{6}$ as a fraction in its lowest terms.

7 What is $0.4\dot{5} - 0.\dot{4}\dot{5}$? Give your answer as a fraction or a decimal.

8 Change all the sevenths ($\frac{1}{7}, \frac{2}{7}, \dots$ up to $\frac{6}{7}$) to decimals.
What do you notice about the answers?
Try the same for the elevenths and the thirteenths. What do you notice?

9 The circumference of a circle divided by its diameter is π.
$\pi = 3.14159\dots$
People occasionally use $3\frac{1}{7}$ as an approximate value.

a What is $3\frac{1}{7}$ as a decimal?

b Can you find a fraction that is a better approximation?

10 Unit fractions are fractions with a numerator of 1.

a How many unit fractions are there with denominators of less than 100?

b How many of these will give recurring decimals?

Explore

◎ $\frac{1}{7}$, when written as a recurring decimal, has six recurring digits

◎ Find the number of recurring digits for other fractions

Investigate further

Decimals

ASSESS

The following exercise tests your understanding of this chapter, with the questions appearing in order of increasing difficulty.

1 Work out the following:

    a 0.4×0.7

    b 2.1×11

    c 0.02×0.235

    d 20.4×4.3

    e 4.02×12.5

    f Mr Burton, the tailor, is cutting cloth for suits. Each suit takes 4.6 m of cloth. How much is needed for 14 suits?

    g One kilogram of nectarines costs £2.95
       How much do 15 kilograms cost?

    h Jane weighed 2.9 kg when she was born. On her first birthday she was 5.2 times as heavy. How heavy was she on her first birthday? Give your answer to the nearest 100 grams.

    i A supermarket stocks boxes of the new breakfast cereal 'Chocobix'. Each packet of 'Chocobix' holds 625 g inside a cardboard box weighing 63 g. The supermarket shelf holds 36 of these packets. What is the total mass, in kilograms, on the shelf?

2 a Convert the following fractions to decimals:

    i $\frac{3}{4}$ **iv** $\frac{7}{16}$

    ii $\frac{1}{8}$ **v** $\frac{14}{25}$

    iii $\frac{4}{5}$

   b Convert the following decimals to fractions:

    i 0.25   **iv** 0.16

    ii 0.375   **v** 0.6875

    iii 0.45

3 a Work out the following:

    i $1.68 \div 0.4$

    ii $220 \div 0.05$

    iii $16.9 \div 1.3$

    iv $6.25 \div 0.25$

    v $49.2 \div 1.2$

b Road Runner travels 3.64 m in 0.7 seconds.
How fast is this in metres per second?

c Naomi sees 54 suspect cells under her microscope in an area of 0.06 cm^2.
How many cells would she expect to find in an area of 1 cm^2?

d A bag of sweets weighing 95 g includes wrappings of 0.5 g.
Each sweet weighs 4.5 g.
How many sweets are in the bag?

4 a Convert the following fractions to decimals without using a calculator:

    i $\frac{1}{3}$ **v** $\frac{7}{15}$

    ii $\frac{2}{7}$ **vi** $\frac{5}{24}$

    iii $\frac{7}{9}$ **vii** $3\frac{7}{12}$

    iv $\frac{6}{11}$

b Use the method shown in Apply **4** question **4** to convert the following decimals to fractions:

    i $0.\dot{7}$

    ii $0.2\dot{7}$

    iii $0.\dot{1}0\dot{1}$

    iv $0.\dot{1}2\dot{3}$

    v $0.5\dot{3}$ (beware: this is harder!)

5 a A rectangular plot, 10.4 m by 7.5 m, is to be sown with grass seed.
The gardener needs 30 g of grass seed each square metre of ground.
Grass seed costs £4.80 per kilogram.
Find:

    i the area of the plot

    ii the mass of grass seed needed

    iii the cost of the seed.

b A beer glass, full of beer, has a mass of 1.43 kg. The glass alone has a mass of 810 g.

    i What is the total mass when the glass is half full of the same beer?

    ii The glass is now filled with a 'heavier' beer. The total weight of the glass and 'heavier' beer is now 1.74 kg. How many times heavier is the new beer compared to the old?

27

c Paul travels from his home in Eastbourne to meet Andrew in Manchester. He travels at 64 miles each hour on average until he stops in a service area. It is 275 miles from Eastbourne to Manchester.

i How far has he travelled after 2 h and 45 min?

ii How far has he still left to travel?

iii Paul now travels at 45 miles each hour on average.
How much longer will his journey take?
(Give your answer in hours and minutes.)

6 a Express $0.5\dot{1}$ as a fraction in its simplest form.

b Express $0.45\dot{1}$ as a fraction in its simplest form.

4 Fractions

OBJECTIVES

D → **Examiners would normally expect students who get a D grade to be able to:**

Do calculations with simple fractions involving subtraction

C → **Examiners would normally expect students who get a C grade also to be able to:**

Do calculations with simple fractions involving division

Do calculations with mixed numbers

What you should already know ...

- Understand fractions including equivalent fractions
- Simplify fractions and arrange them in order
- Calculate fractions of quantities
- Work out one number as a fraction of another number

VOCABULARY

Fraction or **simple fraction** or **common fraction** or **vulgar fraction** – a number written as one whole number over another, for example, $\frac{3}{8}$ (three eighths), which has the same value as $3 \div 8$

Numerator – the number on the top of a fraction

Numerator → $\frac{3}{8}$ ← Denominator

Denominator – the number on the bottom of a fraction

Unit fraction – a fraction with a numerator of 1, for example, $\frac{1}{5}$

Proper fraction – a fraction in which the numerator is smaller than the denominator, for example, $\frac{5}{13}$

Improper fraction or **top-heavy fraction** – a fraction in which the numerator is bigger than the denominator, for example, $\frac{13}{5}$, which is equal to the mixed number $2\frac{3}{5}$

Mixed number or **mixed fraction** – a number made up of a whole number and a fraction, for example, $2\frac{3}{5}$, which is equal to the improper fraction $\frac{13}{5}$

Decimal fraction – a fraction consisting of tenths, hundredths, thousandths, and so on, expressed in a decimal form, for example, 0.65 (6 tenths and 5 hundredths)

Equivalent fraction – a fraction that has the same value as another, for example, $\frac{3}{5}$ is equivalent to $\frac{30}{50}, \frac{6}{10}, \frac{60}{100}, \frac{15}{25}, \frac{1.5}{2.5}, \cdots$

Simplify a fraction or **express a fraction in its simplest form** – to change a fraction to the simplest equivalent fraction; to do this divide the numerator and the denominator by a common factor (this process is called cancelling or reducing or simplifying the fraction)

Learn 1 Adding and subtracting fractions

Examples:

a Calculate $\frac{5}{6} + \frac{3}{4}$

Fractions cannot be added (or subtracted) unless they have the same denominator.

$\frac{5}{6} + \frac{3}{4}$ ← Change both the fractions to twelfths

$= \frac{10}{12} + \frac{9}{12}$ ← When the fractions have both been changed to twelfths, add to find the total number of twelfths

$= \frac{19}{12}$

$= 1\frac{7}{12}$ ← Simplify the answer by writing it as a mixed number

Reminder: $\frac{5}{6} \overset{\times 2}{=} \frac{10}{12}$ and $\frac{3}{4} \overset{\times 3}{=} \frac{9}{12}$
$\,\,\underset{\times 2}{} \qquad\quad \underset{\times 3}{}$

b Calculate $\frac{5}{6} - \frac{3}{4}$

$\frac{5}{6} - \frac{3}{4}$

$= \frac{10}{12} - \frac{9}{12}$

$= \frac{1}{12}$

c Calculate $1\frac{5}{6} + 2\frac{3}{4}$

$1\frac{5}{6} + 2\frac{3}{4}$

$= 1 + \frac{5}{6} + 2 + \frac{3}{4}$

$= 3 + \frac{10}{12} + \frac{9}{12}$

$= 3\frac{19}{12} = 4\frac{7}{12}$

d Calculate $2\frac{1}{6} - \frac{3}{4}$

$2\frac{1}{6} - \frac{3}{4}$

$= 2 + \frac{2}{12} - \frac{9}{12}$

$= 2 - \frac{7}{12}$ ← Change one of the units to twelfths to do this subtraction

$= 1\frac{5}{12}$ $\qquad 2 - \frac{7}{12} = 1 + 1 - \frac{7}{12} = 1 + \frac{12}{12} - \frac{7}{12} = 1\frac{5}{12}$

Apply 1

Questions like this will be on the non-calculator paper so make sure you can do them without using your calculator.

1 Work out: **a** $\frac{3}{4} + \frac{2}{3}$ **b** $\frac{3}{4} - \frac{2}{3}$ **c** $\frac{5}{6} + \frac{2}{5}$ **d** $\frac{5}{6} - \frac{2}{5}$

2 Work out: **a** $3\frac{3}{4} + 1\frac{2}{3}$ **b** $3\frac{3}{4} - 1\frac{2}{3}$ **c** $2\frac{5}{6} + 1\frac{2}{5}$ **d** $2\frac{5}{6} - 1\frac{2}{5}$

3 Work out: **a** $3\frac{2}{3} + 1\frac{3}{4}$ **b** $3\frac{2}{3} - 1\frac{3}{4}$ **c** $2\frac{2}{5} + 1\frac{5}{6}$ **d** $2\frac{2}{5} - 1\frac{5}{6}$

4 Sue says, 'I add up fractions like this: $\frac{5}{6} + \frac{2}{5} = \frac{5+2}{6+5} = \frac{7}{11}$,'
Is Sue right? Explain your answer.

5 Find two fractions with:

a a sum of $1\frac{1}{4}$

b a difference of $1\frac{1}{4}$

c a sum of $3\frac{1}{3}$

d a difference of $3\frac{1}{3}$

6 Get Real!

Anne is making custard, which needs $\frac{1}{3}$ of a cup of sugar.

Then she makes biscuits, which need $\frac{3}{4}$ of a cup of sugar.

Anne only has 1 cup of sugar.
Does she have enough to make the custard and the biscuits?
Show how you got your answer.

7 Get Real!

In America, lengths of fabric for making clothes are measured in
yards and fractions of yards.
A tailor is making a suit for a customer. The jacket needs $2\frac{1}{4}$ yards
of fabric and the trousers need $1\frac{1}{3}$ yards.
The tailor has 4 yards of fabric.
How much will be left over when he has made the jacket and
the trousers?

Explore

A man was riding a camel across a desert, when he came across three young
men arguing. Their father had died, leaving seventeen camels as his sons'
inheritance. The eldest son was to receive half of the camels; the second son,
one-third of the camels and the youngest son, one-ninth of the camels. The sons
asked him how they could divide seventeen camels in this way.

The man added his camel to the 17. Then, he gave $\frac{1}{2}$ of the camels to the eldest
son, $\frac{1}{3}$ of the camels to the second son and $\frac{1}{9}$ of the camels to the youngest son.
Having solved the problem, the stranger mounted his own camel and rode away.

How does this work?

Investigate further

Learn 2 Multiplying and dividing fractions

Examples:

a Calculate:

  i $12 \times \frac{1}{3}$ **ii** $12 \times \frac{2}{3}$ **iii** $\frac{3}{4} \times \frac{2}{3}$

  i $12 \times \frac{1}{3}$ ⟵ — Multiplying by $\frac{1}{3}$ is the same as dividing by 3

     $= \frac{12}{3}$

     $= 4$

  ii $12 \times \frac{2}{3}$ ⟵ Multiplying by $\frac{2}{3}$ is the same as dividing by 3 and multiplying by 2

     $= \frac{24}{3}$

     $= 8$

  iii $\frac{3}{4} \times \frac{2}{3}$

     $= \frac{3 \times 2}{4 \times 3}$

     $= \frac{6}{12}$

     $= \frac{1}{2}$

b Calculate:

  i $8 \div \frac{1}{3}$ **ii** $8 \div \frac{2}{3}$ **iii** $\frac{3}{4} \div \frac{2}{3}$

  i $8 \div \frac{1}{3}$ ⟵ — Dividing 8 by a third means finding how many thirds there are in 8.

     $= 8 \times \frac{3}{1}$ There are three thirds in each whole, so there

     $= 24$ are 8×3 thirds in 8

  ii $8 \div \frac{2}{3}$ ⟵ The number of two-thirds in 8 is half the number of thirds in 8

     $= 8 \times \frac{3}{2}$ Dividing by $\frac{2}{3}$ is the same as multiplying by $\frac{3}{2}$

     $= 12$

  iii $\frac{3}{4} \div \frac{2}{3}$

     $= \frac{3}{4} \times \frac{3}{2}$ ⟵ Dividing by a fraction is the same as multiplying by the reciprocal (upside-down) fraction

     $= \frac{3 \times 3}{4 \times 2}$

     $= \frac{9}{8}$

     $= 1\frac{1}{8}$

Apply 2

1 Work out:

a $18 \times \frac{1}{3}$ **c** $35 \times \frac{1}{7}$ **e** $40 \times \frac{2}{5}$ **g** $24 \times \frac{5}{8}$

b $28 \times \frac{1}{4}$ **d** $40 \times \frac{1}{5}$ **f** $12 \times \frac{3}{4}$ **h** $42 \times \frac{5}{6}$

2 Work out:

a $\frac{4}{5} \times \frac{1}{2}$ **c** $\frac{5}{6} \times \frac{1}{4}$ **e** $\frac{5}{8} \times \frac{3}{5}$ **g** $\frac{11}{12} \times \frac{4}{5}$

b $\frac{3}{8} \times \frac{1}{3}$ **d** $\frac{9}{10} \times \frac{1}{6}$ **f** $\frac{8}{9} \times \frac{3}{4}$ **h** $\frac{9}{10} \times \frac{2}{3}$

3 Work out:

a $18 \div \frac{1}{3}$ **c** $6 \div \frac{1}{5}$ **e** $18 \div \frac{2}{3}$ **g** $28 \div \frac{4}{5}$

b $5 \div \frac{1}{4}$ **d** $10 \div \frac{1}{8}$ **f** $12 \div \frac{3}{4}$ **h** $35 \div \frac{5}{6}$

4 Work out:

a $\frac{7}{8} \div \frac{1}{2}$ **c** $\frac{4}{9} \div \frac{2}{5}$ **e** $\frac{1}{3} \div \frac{1}{3}$ **g** $\frac{3}{5} \div \frac{7}{10}$

b $\frac{1}{6} \div \frac{2}{3}$ **d** $\frac{2}{7} \div \frac{2}{3}$ **f** $\frac{1}{3} \div \frac{1}{5}$ **h** $\frac{11}{12} \div \frac{3}{4}$

5 Paula is working out $\frac{4}{15} \div \frac{3}{8}$

She says, 'I can cancel the 4 into the 8 and the 3 into the 15.'

Then she writes down $\frac{1}{5} \div \frac{1}{2} = \frac{1}{5} \times \frac{2}{1} = \frac{2}{5}$

Is this correct? Explain your answer.

6 Ali says, 'This is how to divide fractions: $\frac{5}{6} \div \frac{2}{5} = \frac{6}{5} \times \frac{2}{5} = \frac{12}{25}$,'

Is Ali right? Explain your answer.

7 Without working out the answers, say which of these gives an answer greater than 1:

$\frac{9}{10} \times \frac{4}{5}$ or $\frac{9}{10} \div \frac{4}{5}$?

Give a reason for your answer.

8 Write down two fractions that:

a multiply to give 1   **b** divide to give 1.

9 Get Real!

Two thirds of the teachers in a school are women and three quarters of these are over 40. What fraction of the teachers in the school are women over 40?

10 Get Real!

Seven eighths of the members of the running club train on Wednesday evening and four fifths of them are male. What fraction of the members are males who train on Wednesday evenings?

Fraction

The following exercise tests your understanding of this chapter, with the questions appearing in order of increasing difficulty.

1 a Scrooge collects money.

$\frac{3}{10}$ of his fortune is in brass coins, $\frac{8}{15}$ is in silver and the rest is in notes.

What fraction of Scrooge's fortune is in notes?

b In the 4×100 m relay, the first runner took $\frac{1}{5}$ of his team's total time.

The second runner took $\frac{7}{30}$ of their total time.

The third runner took $\frac{3}{10}$ of their total time.

  i What fraction of their time was taken by the fourth member of the team?

  ii Which team member ran the fastest leg of the race?

  iii Which team member ran the slowest leg of the race?

c Delia is cooking. She has a $1\frac{1}{2}$ kg bag of flour and needs $\frac{3}{8}$ of it in a recipe. What fraction of a kilogram does she need and what is this in grams?

d S. Crumpy has an orchard.

The orchard contains $4\frac{1}{3}$ hectares of apple trees.

Today he needs to treat $\frac{4}{5}$ of the area for disease prevention.

What area does he need to treat?

e In a football match the goalkeeper kicked the ball from the goal line for $\frac{5}{8}$ of the length of the pitch and a player then kicked it a further $\frac{5}{24}$

The length of the pitch is 90 yards.
How far is the ball from the opposing goal line?

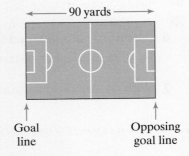

Goal line   Opposing goal line

2 a Work out the following:

  i $6\frac{3}{7} + 3\frac{6}{7}$ **iii** $9\frac{4}{5} + 6\frac{3}{8}$ **v** $11\frac{2}{7} - 6\frac{4}{5}$ **vii** $10 \div \frac{2}{3}$

  ii $8\frac{1}{4} - 4\frac{5}{8}$ **iv** $7\frac{5}{8} - 3\frac{1}{4}$ **vi** $\frac{2}{3} \times \frac{5}{6}$ **viii** $3\frac{1}{5} \div 1\frac{3}{5}$

b i Titus Lines, the fisherman, catches one fish of mass $2\frac{1}{3}$ kg and another of mass $3\frac{1}{4}$ kg. What total mass of fish does he catch?

  ii What is the perimeter of a triangle of sides $2\frac{1}{4}$, $3\frac{1}{5}$ and $4\frac{3}{10}$ inches?

  iii A can holds $2\frac{8}{9}$ litres of oil. Hakim uses $1\frac{4}{15}$ litres. How much is left?

  iv Deirdre drops Ken off at work after driving from home for $4\frac{5}{12}$ miles. She drives $7\frac{1}{4}$ miles altogether to her own place of work. How far is Ken's workplace from Deirdre's workplace?

  v Milo is $1\frac{2}{5}$ metres tall. He is $\frac{3}{8}$ metre taller than Fizz. How tall is Fizz?

5 Surds

OBJECTIVES

A ▶ **Examiners would normally expect students who get an A grade to be able to:**

Rationalise the denominator of a surd, such as $\dfrac{2}{\sqrt{5}}$

A* ▶ **Examiners would normally expect students who get an A* grade also to be able to:**

Simplify surds, such as write $(3 - \sqrt{5})^2$ in the form $a + b\sqrt{5}$

What you should already know ...

■ Squares of numbers up to 15

■ Multiplying fractions, and converting fractions to decimals and vice versa

■ Prime factors and the expression of numbers as products of prime factors

VOCABULARY

Rational number – a number that can be expressed in the form $\frac{p}{q}$ where p and q are both integers, for example, $1(= \frac{1}{1})$, $2\frac{1}{3}(= \frac{7}{3})$, $\frac{3}{5}$, $0.\dot{1}(= \frac{1}{9})$; rational numbers, when written as decimals, are terminating decimals or recurring decimals

Irrational number – a number that is not an integer and cannot be written as a fraction, for example, $\sqrt{2}, \sqrt{3}, \sqrt{5}$ and π; irrational numbers, when expressed as decimals, are infinite, non-recurring decimals

Surd – a number containing an irrational root, for example, $\sqrt{2}$ or $3 + 2\sqrt{7}$

Learn 1 Simplifying surds

Examples: **a** Are these numbers rational or irrational?

    i $\sqrt{7}$ **ii** $\sqrt{16}$ **iii** $\dfrac{\pi}{2}$ **iv** $\dfrac{\pi}{2\pi}$

    i $\sqrt{7}$ is irrational.   **iii** $\dfrac{\pi}{2}$ is irrational because π is irrational.

    ii $\sqrt{16} = 4$; it is rational.   **iv** $\dfrac{\pi}{2\pi} = \dfrac{1}{2}$; it is rational.

Do not forget to simplify if you can

    b Simplify these.

    i $\sqrt{6} \times \sqrt{12}$ **ii** $3\sqrt{2} + \sqrt{32}$ **iii** $\dfrac{\sqrt{40}}{\sqrt{5}}$

    i $\sqrt{6} \times \sqrt{12}$

$= \sqrt{6 \times 12}$ ← $\sqrt{a} \times \sqrt{b} = \sqrt{ab}$

$= \sqrt{72}$

$= \sqrt{36 \times 2}$

$= \sqrt{36} \times \sqrt{2}$ ← $\sqrt{ab} = \sqrt{a} \times \sqrt{b}$

$= 6\sqrt{2}$ ← $\sqrt{36} = 6$

Remember:

$\sqrt{ab} = \sqrt{a} \times \sqrt{b}$

$\sqrt{\dfrac{a}{b}} = \dfrac{\sqrt{a}}{\sqrt{b}}$

$a\sqrt{c} + b\sqrt{c} = (a+b)\sqrt{c}$

$a\sqrt{c} - b\sqrt{c} = (a-b)\sqrt{c}$

    ii $3\sqrt{2} + \sqrt{32}$

$= 3\sqrt{2} + \sqrt{16 \times 2}$

$= 3\sqrt{2} + \sqrt{16} \times \sqrt{2}$

$= 3\sqrt{2} + 4\sqrt{2}$

$= 7\sqrt{2}$ ← $a\sqrt{c} + b\sqrt{c} = (a+b)\sqrt{c}$

    iii $\dfrac{\sqrt{40}}{\sqrt{5}}$

$= \sqrt{\dfrac{40}{5}}$ ← $\dfrac{\sqrt{a}}{\sqrt{b}} = \sqrt{\dfrac{a}{b}}$

$= \sqrt{8}$

$= 2\sqrt{2}$

Apply 1

1 Write these numbers in the form $\dfrac{a}{b}$, giving your answers in their lowest terms.

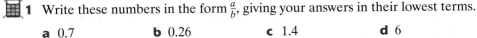

    a 0.7   **b** 0.26   **c** 1.4   **d** 6   **e** $0.\dot{1}\dot{8}$

 **2** Which of these are rational, and which are irrational? Give a reason for your answer.

a $\sqrt{24}$	**f** $\sqrt{6}$	**k** $\sqrt{3} \times \sqrt{3}$	**p** $(\sqrt{16})^3$
b $\sqrt{25}$	**g** $\sqrt{6} \times \sqrt{6}$	**l** $\sqrt{3} \times \sqrt{12}$	**q** $\sqrt{(3^2)}$
c $\dfrac{4}{11}$	**h** $6 \times \sqrt{6}$	**m** $(\sqrt{5})^2$	**r** $\sqrt[3]{(8^2)}$
d $\dfrac{\sqrt{4}}{11}$	**i** $\sqrt{3}$	**n** $(\sqrt[3]{7})^3$	
e $\dfrac{4}{\sqrt{11}}$	**j** $\sqrt{3} \times 3$	**o** $(\sqrt{11})^3$	

3 Get Real!

A draughtsman is trying to draw a square with an area of 2 m². However, he knows about surds, and realises his square needs to have a side of $\sqrt{2}$ m, which is irrational. This means he cannot measure the length exactly, as irrational numbers have no exact fraction or decimal equivalent.

He suddenly has a brilliant idea how he can draw his square without having to measure an irrational length. Can you think how he might have done it?

> **HINT** He started with a bigger square, with double the area.

4 Charlotte and Jack are having an argument about square roots.
Charlotte says that $\sqrt{90}$ must be irrational because all square roots are irrational.
Jack says she is wrong; $\sqrt{9} = 3$, so $\sqrt{90} = 30$.
Who is wrong? Explain how you know.

5 Write down three irrational numbers between 2 and 3.

6 Simplify these.

a $\sqrt{20}$	**c** $\sqrt{32}$	**e** $\sqrt{80}$	**g** $\sqrt{108}$
b $\sqrt{45}$	**d** $\sqrt{500}$	**f** $\sqrt{98}$	**h** $\sqrt{75}$

7 Simplify these.

a $2\sqrt{3} + 3\sqrt{3}$	**c** $3\sqrt{5} - 2\sqrt{5}$	**e** $\sqrt{18} - \sqrt{8}$	**g** $\sqrt{72} + \sqrt{18}$
b $3\sqrt{2} + \sqrt{2}$	**d** $\sqrt{20} + \sqrt{5}$	**f** $3\sqrt{7} - \sqrt{28}$	**h** $\sqrt{8} + 3\sqrt{2} - \sqrt{50}$

8 Bobby says $\sqrt{10} + \sqrt{15} = \sqrt{25} = 5$.
Jen works it out differently, but gets the same answer.
She says $\sqrt{10} + \sqrt{15} = \sqrt{2} \times \sqrt{5} + \sqrt{3} \times \sqrt{5} = (\sqrt{2} + \sqrt{3}) \times \sqrt{5} = \sqrt{5} \times \sqrt{5} = 5$.
But Ed knows that $\sqrt{10}$ and $\sqrt{15}$ are both greater than 3, so the answer must be more than 6.

a What did Bobby do wrong?

b Where did Jen go wrong?

9 Simplify:

a $\sqrt{3} \times \sqrt{12}$	**c** $\sqrt{18} \times \sqrt{2}$	**e** $\sqrt{10} \times 3\sqrt{5}$	**g** $2\sqrt{5} \times \sqrt{10}$
b $\sqrt{10} \times \sqrt{20}$	**d** $2\sqrt{3} \times \sqrt{6}$	**f** $5\sqrt{6} \times 2\sqrt{3}$	**h** $7\sqrt{7} \times 2\sqrt{7}$

10 Simplify:

a $\dfrac{\sqrt{12}}{\sqrt{3}}$ 　　　 d $\dfrac{\sqrt{88}}{2}$ 　　　 g $\dfrac{6\sqrt{10}}{2\sqrt{5}}$ 　　　 j $\dfrac{2\sqrt{21}}{8\sqrt{3}}$

b $\sqrt{\dfrac{81}{16}}$ 　　　 e $\dfrac{3\sqrt{6}}{\sqrt{3}}$ 　　　 h $\dfrac{8\sqrt{30}}{4\sqrt{5}}$ 　　　 k $\dfrac{2\sqrt{10}}{10\sqrt{2}}$

c $\sqrt{\dfrac{45}{20}}$ 　　　 f $\dfrac{5\sqrt{6}}{\sqrt{2}}$ 　　　 i $\dfrac{2\sqrt{5}}{4}$ 　　　 l $\dfrac{6\sqrt{21}}{15\sqrt{7}}$

11 Dan says that $\dfrac{\sqrt{20}}{5} = \sqrt{4} = 2$.

Is Dan correct?
Give a reason for your answer.

12 Get Real!

Tessell Ltd make wall tiles. They make two different sizes of square tile and one rectangle, to tessellate as shown. The large square has an area of 30 cm^2, and the small square has an area of 15 cm^2.

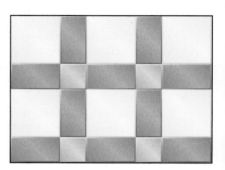

a What are the exact dimensions (length and width) of the rectangular tile?
Give your answers as surds in their simplest form.

b What is the area of the rectangular tile?
Give your answers as surds in their simplest form.

13 a Find two irrational numbers that multiply together to make a rational number.

b Find two irrational numbers that, when divided, give the answer 2.

14 Put the numbers below into pairs with the same value.

a $2\sqrt{2} + \sqrt{2}$ 　　　 **c** $\dfrac{6\sqrt{3}}{3}$ 　　　 **e** $\dfrac{6\sqrt{3}}{\sqrt{3}}$ 　　　 **g** $\sqrt{\dfrac{12}{2}}$

b $\sqrt{3} \times \sqrt{2}$ 　　　 **d** $\sqrt{18}$ 　　　 **f** $\dfrac{\sqrt{24}}{\sqrt{2}}$ 　　　 **h** $\dfrac{\sqrt{72}}{\sqrt{2}}$

15 Show that:

a $\sqrt{18} \times \sqrt{2} = 6$ 　　　 **d** $\sqrt{\dfrac{90}{10}} = 3$ 　　　 **g** $\dfrac{\sqrt{60}}{2} = \sqrt{15}$

b $\sqrt{72} = 6\sqrt{2}$ 　　　 **e** $\sqrt{2} \times \sqrt{3} \times \sqrt{4} \times \sqrt{5} \times \sqrt{6} = 12\sqrt{5}$ 　　　 **h** $5\sqrt{3} - \sqrt{3} = \sqrt{48}$

c $3\sqrt{2} \times \sqrt{8} = 12$ 　　　 **f** $\dfrac{3\sqrt{5} + 2\sqrt{5}}{5} = \sqrt{5}$ 　　　 **i** $\sqrt{80} - \sqrt{20} = 2\sqrt{5}$

16 Write $\sqrt{15} \times \sqrt{5}$ in the form $a\sqrt{b}$, where a and b are both prime numbers.

17 a Show that $(\sqrt{12} - \sqrt{3})^2 = 3$.

b In part **a** the answer was 3, a rational number, but not many expressions of the form $(\sqrt{a} - \sqrt{b})^2$, where a and b are irrational, give a rational answer. Expand $(\sqrt{a} - \sqrt{b})^2$, and find another example of $(\sqrt{a} - \sqrt{b})^2$, where a and b are irrational, which gives a rational answer.

18 Simplify these.

a $\sqrt{2}(3 + \sqrt{2})$

b $\sqrt{3}(2 + \sqrt{12})$

c $(1 + \sqrt{2})(2 + \sqrt{2})$

d $(3 - \sqrt{2})(1 - \sqrt{2})$

e $(\sqrt{3} + 2)(\sqrt{3} - 2)$

f $(5 - \sqrt{7})^2$

g $(a + \sqrt{3})(a - \sqrt{3})$

h $(c + \sqrt{d})(c - \sqrt{d})$

Explore

Look at these four numbers:

| $5\sqrt{2}$ | $5 - \sqrt{2}$ | $3 + \sqrt{2}$ | $5 + \sqrt{2}$ |

◎ Find a pair of numbers in the list with a rational sum and a rational product

◎ Find a pair of numbers in the list with an irrational sum and an irrational product

◎ Find a pair of numbers in the list with a rational sum and an irrational product

◎ Find a pair of numbers in the list with an irrational sum and a rational product

Make up your own starting numbers

Investigate further

Learn 2   Rationalising the denominator of a surd

Examples:

Rationalise and simplify these.

Rationalise means remove the square roots

a $\dfrac{\sqrt{3}}{\sqrt{2}}$ **b** $\dfrac{5}{2\sqrt{3}}$

Multiply the numerator and denominator by the irrational part of the denominator

a $\dfrac{\sqrt{3}}{\sqrt{2}}$

$= \dfrac{\sqrt{3} \times \sqrt{2}}{\sqrt{2} \times \sqrt{2}}$

$= \dfrac{\sqrt{6}}{2}$

b $\dfrac{5}{2\sqrt{3}}$

$= \dfrac{5 \times \sqrt{3}}{2\sqrt{3} \times \sqrt{3}}$

$= \dfrac{5\sqrt{3}}{2 \times 3}$

$= \dfrac{5\sqrt{3}}{6}$

You can multiply surds together, for example,

$\sqrt{a} \times \sqrt{a} = a$ (as $\sqrt{a} \times \sqrt{a} = \sqrt{a \times a} = \sqrt{a^2} = a$)

$(a + \sqrt{b})(a - \sqrt{b}) = a^2 - b$ (as $(a + \sqrt{b})(a - \sqrt{b}) = a^2 - a\sqrt{b} + a\sqrt{b} - b = a^2 - b$)

Apply 2

1 Simplify:

 a $\dfrac{\sqrt{12}}{\sqrt{3}}$ **b** $\dfrac{\sqrt{7}}{\sqrt{28}}$ **c** $\dfrac{2\sqrt{3}}{\sqrt{27}}$ **d** $\dfrac{3\sqrt{5}}{\sqrt{20}}$

2 Rationalise and simplify:

 a $\dfrac{5}{\sqrt{3}}$ **d** $\dfrac{5}{\sqrt{10}}$ **g** $\dfrac{3}{\sqrt{3}}$ **j** $\dfrac{3}{2\sqrt{3}}$

 b $\dfrac{2}{\sqrt{7}}$ **e** $\dfrac{9}{\sqrt{3}}$ **h** $\dfrac{30}{\sqrt{15}}$ **k** $\dfrac{7}{4\sqrt{5}}$

 c $\dfrac{1}{\sqrt{11}}$ **f** $\dfrac{20}{\sqrt{5}}$ **i** $\dfrac{8}{\sqrt{2}}$ **l** $\dfrac{9}{4\sqrt{3}}$

3 Darren says $\sqrt{\dfrac{6}{18}} = \sqrt{\dfrac{1}{3}} = \sqrt{\dfrac{1 \times \sqrt{3}}{3 \times \sqrt{3}}} = \dfrac{\sqrt{3}}{3\sqrt{3}} = \dfrac{1}{3}$

 Pablo says $\sqrt{\dfrac{6}{18}} = \dfrac{\sqrt{6}}{\sqrt{18}} = \dfrac{\sqrt{6}}{\sqrt{9} \times \sqrt{2}} = \dfrac{\sqrt{6}}{3\sqrt{2}} = \dfrac{\sqrt{2}}{\sqrt{2}} = 1$

 a Find Darren's mistake.

 b Find Pablo's mistake.

 c Work out the correct answer.

4 **Get Real!**

 A room has a length which is exactly $\sqrt{2}$ times its width.
 The length is 10 m.

 a What is the width? Give your answer as a surd
  (with a rational denominator).

 b What is the area?

5 a Write five fractions like $\dfrac{2}{\sqrt{2}}, \dfrac{5}{\sqrt{5}}$ and so on, where the denominator is
  the square root of the numerator.

 b Rationalise the denominators of the fractions you wrote in part **a**.

 c Use algebra to generalise what happens when you rationalise the
  denominator of $\dfrac{a}{\sqrt{a}}$

 d Rationalise the denominator of $\dfrac{ab}{\sqrt{a}}$

6 Copy and find your way through this maze, only occupying spaces where the answer is correct.

Start →	$\dfrac{2}{\sqrt{3}} = \dfrac{2\sqrt{3}}{3}$ ✓	$\dfrac{2}{\sqrt{5}} = \dfrac{\sqrt{5}}{2}$	$\dfrac{\sqrt{4}}{3} = \dfrac{2}{3}$	End
$\dfrac{1}{\sqrt{2}} = \sqrt{2}$ ✗	$\dfrac{4}{\sqrt{6}} = \dfrac{2\sqrt{6}}{3}$	$\dfrac{a}{\sqrt{2a}} = \sqrt{a}$	$\dfrac{6}{\sqrt{3}} = 2\sqrt{3}$	$\dfrac{2}{1+\sqrt{4}} = \dfrac{2}{5}$
$\dfrac{4}{\sqrt{2}} = 2\sqrt{2}$	$\dfrac{1}{\sqrt{5}} = \dfrac{\sqrt{5}}{5}$	$\dfrac{7}{\sqrt{2}} = 7\sqrt{2}$	$\dfrac{a}{\sqrt{b}} = \dfrac{a\sqrt{b}}{b}$	$\dfrac{7}{\sqrt{7}} = \sqrt{7}$
$\dfrac{3}{\sqrt{3}} = \sqrt{3}$	$\dfrac{1}{5\sqrt{2}} = \dfrac{5\sqrt{2}}{2}$	$\dfrac{2a}{\sqrt{2a}} = 2\sqrt{a}$	$\dfrac{3}{2\sqrt{3}} = \dfrac{\sqrt{3}}{3}$	$\dfrac{12}{\sqrt{3}} = 4\sqrt{3}$
$\dfrac{3a}{\sqrt{a}} = 3\sqrt{a}$	$\dfrac{5}{\sqrt{2}} = \dfrac{5\sqrt{2}}{2}$	$\dfrac{11}{\sqrt{11}} = \dfrac{\sqrt{11}}{11}$	$\dfrac{4}{\sqrt{36}} = \dfrac{2}{3}$	$\dfrac{5}{\sqrt{10}} = \dfrac{\sqrt{10}}{2}$
$\dfrac{3}{\sqrt{2}} = \sqrt{2}$	$\dfrac{9}{\sqrt{6}} = \dfrac{3\sqrt{6}}{2}$	$\dfrac{a}{\sqrt{50}} = \dfrac{a\sqrt{2}}{10}$	$\dfrac{9}{\sqrt{3}} = 3\sqrt{3}$	$\dfrac{1}{\sqrt{50}} = \dfrac{\sqrt{50}}{25}$

Explore

◎ Take a sheet of A4 paper

Measure its length and width – be as accurate as you can

Divide the length by the width

Write down the answer

What is important about this number?

◎ Do the same for pieces of A3 and A5 paper

What do you notice about your answers?

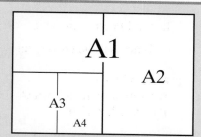

Investigate further

Explore

◎ Write down two numbers, a and b, such that $a = b^3$

◎ Show that, for your a and b, $\dfrac{a}{\sqrt{b}} = b^2\sqrt{b}$

Investigate further

Surds

The following exercise tests your understanding of this chapter, with the questions appearing in order of increasing difficulty.

1 a Which of these numbers are rational and which are irrational? How can you tell?

$$\sqrt{5} \qquad \sqrt{9} \qquad \frac{\sqrt{16}}{7} \qquad \sqrt{\frac{16}{7}} \qquad \frac{\sqrt{63}}{\sqrt{7}}$$

b Square these numbers.

  i $\sqrt{8}$ **iv** $\sqrt{x}$ **vii** $\sqrt{3} \times \sqrt{8}$

  ii $\sqrt{13}$ **v** $2\sqrt{3}$ **viii** $\sqrt{y} \times \sqrt{z}$

  iii $\sqrt{25}$ **vi** $5\sqrt{a}$

2 a Write, in their simplest form:

  i $\sqrt{8}$ **iii** $\sqrt{98}$ **v** $5\sqrt{50}$

  ii $\sqrt{45}$ **iv** $4\sqrt{18}$

b Express these as square roots of a single number, for example, $3\sqrt{7} = \sqrt{9} \times \sqrt{7} = \sqrt{63}$.

  i $2\sqrt{3}$ **iii** $4\sqrt{7}$ **v** $10\sqrt{2}$

  ii $3\sqrt{5}$ **iv** $2\sqrt{11}$

3 a Rationalise these expressions.

  i $\dfrac{2}{\sqrt{2}}$ **ii** $\dfrac{3}{\sqrt{5}}$ **iii** $\dfrac{4}{\sqrt{7}}$

b The sides containing the right angle in a right-angled triangle are 7 cm and 5 cm. What is the *exact* length of the hypotenuse?

4 a One well-known irrational number is not written with a $\sqrt{}$ sign. What number is it?

b Write in the form $a + b\sqrt{c}$:

  i $(\sqrt{2} + 3)^2$ **iv** $(\sqrt{3} + \sqrt{2})(\sqrt{3} - \sqrt{2})$

  ii $(\sqrt{5} - 4)^2$ **v** $(2\sqrt{5} + 3\sqrt{7})(3\sqrt{5} - 2\sqrt{7})$

  iii $(1 + \sqrt{2})(2 - \sqrt{2})$

5 A rectangle measures 15 m by 3 m.

  a Find the exact length of the side of a square with the same area.

  b Find the radius of a circle with the same area. Express your answers in their simplest form.

6 Indices and standard form

D   **Examiners would normally expect students who get a D grade to be able to:**

Use the terms square, positive square root, negative square root, cube and cube root

Recall integer squares from 2×2 to 15×15 and the corresponding square roots

Recall the cubes of 2, 3, 4, 5 and 10

C   **Examiners would normally expect students who get a C grade also to be able to:**

Use index notation and index laws for positive and negative powers such as $w^3 \times w^5$ and $\dfrac{w^3}{w^7}$

B   **Examiners would normally expect students who get a B grade also to be able to:**

Use index notation and index laws for positive and negative powers such as $3w^3y \times 2w^5y^2$ and $\dfrac{8w^5z}{2w^3z^2}$

Convert between numbers in ordinary and standard index form

Use standard index form with and without a calculator

A   **Examiners would normally expect students who get an A grade also to be able to:**

Use index notation and index laws for fractional powers such as $16^{\frac{1}{4}}$

A*   **Examiners would normally expect students who get an A* grade also to be able to:**

Use index notation and index laws for fractional powers such as $16^{\frac{3}{4}}$

What you should already know ...

■ Calculate squares and square roots (with and without the use of a calculator)

■ Calculate cubes and cube roots (with and without the use of a calculator)

■ Use function keys on a calculator for powers, roots and reciprocals

VOCABULARY

Square number – a square number is the outcome when a whole number is multiplied by itself

Cube number – a cube number is the outcome when a whole number is multiplied by itself then multiplied by itself again

Square root – the square root of a number such as 16 is a number whose outcome is 16 when multiplied by itself

Cube root – the cube root of a number such as 125 is a number whose outcome is 125 when multiplied by itself then multiplied by itself again

Index or **power** or **exponent** – the index tells you how many times the base number is to be multiplied by itself

Index
5^3
Base

So $5^3 = 5 \times 5 \times 5$

Indices – the plural of index

Standard form – standard form is a shorthand way of writing very large and very small numbers; standard form numbers are always written as:

A power of 10

$$A \times 10^n$$

A must be at least 1 but less than 10

Learn 1   Rules of indices

Examples:

a Work out 5^3

b Work out:

  i $6^3 \times 6^2$ **ii** $a^3 \times a^2$ **iii** $6a^3 \times 3a^2$

c Work out:

  i $\dfrac{2^5}{2^2}$ **ii** $\dfrac{a^5}{a^2}$ **iii** $\dfrac{15a^5}{3a^2}$

d Work out:

  i $(3^5)^2$ **ii** $(a^5)^2$ **iii** $(6a^5)^2$

a

Index (or power or exponent)

5^3

Base

So $5^3 = 5 \times 5 \times 5 = 125$

The index (or power or exponent) tells you how many times the base number is to be multiplied by itself

You can use the $\boxed{x^y}$ button for indices on your calculator

		i	**ii**	**iii**
		Number	**Algebra**	**Higher algebra**
b		$6^3 \times 6^2$	$a^3 \times a^2$	$6a^3 \times 3a^2$
		$= 6^{(3+2)}$	$= a^{(3+2)}$	$= 6 \times a^3 \times 3 \times a^2$
		$= 6^5$	$= a^5$	$= 6 \times 3 \times a^3 \times a^2$
				$= 18 \times a^{(3+2)}$
				$= 18a^5$
c		$\dfrac{2^5}{2^2}$	$\dfrac{a^5}{a^2}$	$\dfrac{15a^5}{3a^2}$
		$= 2^5 \div 2^2$	$= a^5 \div a^2$	$= \dfrac{15}{3} \times a^5 \div a^2$
		$= 2^{(5-2)}$	$= a^{(5-2)}$	$= 5 \times a^{(5-2)}$
		$= 2^3$	$= a^3$	$= 5a^3$
d		$(3^5)^2$	$(a^5)^2$	$(6a^5)^2$
		$= 3^{(5 \times 2)}$	$= a^{(5 \times 2)}$	$= 6^2 \times (a^5)^2$
		$= 3^{10}$	$= a^{10}$	$= 36 \times a^{(5 \times 2)}$
				$= 36 \times a^{10}$
				$= 36a^{10}$

Rules of indices

In general
$a^m \times a^n = a^{m+n}$

$a^m \div a^n = a^{m-n}$

$(a^m)^n = a^{m \times n}$

$a^{-m} = \dfrac{1}{a^m}$

$a^0 = 1$

$a^{\frac{1}{n}} = \sqrt[n]{a}$

(that is, the nth root of a
so $a^{\frac{1}{2}} = \sqrt{a}$ and $a^{\frac{1}{3}} = \sqrt[3]{a}$ etc)

Apply 1

1 Find the value of each of the following.

    a 1.5^2 **c** $\sqrt{225}$ **e** $\sqrt[3]{-64}$

    b 10^3 **d** $\sqrt[3]{1}$

2 Calculate: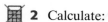

    a $3^2 + 4^2$ **c** $10^3 - \sqrt{100}$ **e** $\sqrt{5^2 + 12^2}$

    b $2^3 \times 3^2$ **d** $\sqrt{225} - \sqrt[3]{125}$ **f** $\sqrt{3^2 \times 5^2}$

3 Neil says -3^2 is 9.
Andrea says -3^2 is -9.
Who is correct?
Give a reason for your answer.

4 Write the following numbers in index notation.

    a $5 \times 5 \times 5 \times 5$ **c** 13×13 **e** $\dfrac{1}{5}$

    b $2 \times 2 \times 2 \times 2 \times 2 \times 2 \times 2$ **d** 8 **f** $\dfrac{1}{25}$

5 Find the value of each of the following.

    a 7^2 **e** 4^6 **i** 3^{-1}

    b 2^5 **f** 12^0 **j** 2^{-3}

    c 3^4 **g** 1^2 **k** 4^{-6}

    d 5^1 **h** 1^{100} **l** 100^{-1}

6 Find the value of each of the following.

a 2^6 **d** 8^6 **g** $2^6 + 6^2$

b 2^{10} **e** 9^4 **h** $5^5 \times 10^{-4}$

c 3^5 **f** $2^{11} - 5^3$ **i** $10^8 - 10^6$

7 Simplify the following numbers, giving your answers in index form.

a $5^6 \times 5^2$ **d** $7^{10} \div 7^5$ **g** $\dfrac{4^2 \times 4^3}{4^6}$

b $12^8 \times 12^3$ **e** $3^7 \div 3^{10}$

c $\dfrac{4^7}{4^3}$ **f** $(9^2)^5$

8 Calculate:

a $49^{\frac{1}{2}}$ **e** $-8^{\frac{2}{3}}$ **i** $(-125)^{\frac{2}{3}}$

b $121^{\frac{1}{2}}$ **f** $(-8)^{\frac{2}{3}}$ **j** $1^{\frac{1}{3}}$

c $64^{\frac{1}{3}}$ **g** $32^{\frac{2}{5}}$ **k** $1^{-\frac{1}{3}}$

d $8^{\frac{2}{3}}$ **h** $4^{-\frac{1}{2}}$

9 Say whether these statements are true or false.
Give a reason for your answer.

a $6^2 = 12$ **d** $16^{-\frac{1}{2}} = -4$ **g** $10^{50} \times 10^{50} = 10^{100}$

b $1^3 = 1$ **e** $\dfrac{2^{10}}{4^5} = 1$ **h** $(-216)^{\frac{1}{3}} = -6$

c $1^{-\frac{1}{2}} = -1$ **f** $3^4 + 3^5 = 3^9$ **i** $1\,000\,000^0 = 0$

10 Use your calculator to work out each of the following.

a 60^2 **b** $16^{-0.5}$ **c** $729^{1.5}$ **d** $256^{-0.25}$

11 Put these in order, starting with the smallest.

$64^{\frac{1}{3}}, \ 64^{\frac{1}{4}}, \ (1/64)^{\frac{1}{2}}, \ 64^{-\frac{1}{3}}$

12 Simplify the following, giving your answers in index form.

a $x^6 \times x^2$ **c** $\dfrac{a^7}{a^3}$ **e** $q^7 \div q^{10}$

b $e^8 \times e^3$ **d** $p^{10} \div p^5$ **f** $(b^2)^5$

13 Simplify the following.

a $2x^2 \times 3x^5$ **d** $(4b^2)^3$

b $\dfrac{3a^6}{6a^2}$ **e** $\dfrac{c^6 \times c^9}{c^5}$

c $5c^2 \times 2c^7$ **f** $\dfrac{5c^2 \times 2c^7}{c^6}$

> **HINT**
> Write $2x^2 \times 3x^5$ as $2 \times x^2 \times 3 \times x^5$
> $= 2 \times 3 \times x^2 \times x^5$
> $= 6 \times x^2 \times x^5$
> $= 6x^7$

14 a Find the product of $7xy^2$ and $3x^4y^3$.

b Write down five other expressions that give the same product as your answer in part **a**.

HINT Write $7xy^2$ as $7x \times y^2$.

15 The number 64 can be written as 8^2 in index form.
Write down five other ways that 64 can be written in index form.

Explore

◎ Manjula says that 1^n is always 1
Is Manjula correct?

◎ Try different values of n, for example, positive and negative

Investigate further

Explore

◎ Alan notices that $\sqrt{4} \times \sqrt{9} = \sqrt{4 \times 9}$

◎ Investigate for other numbers

◎ What happens if you divide the two numbers?

Investigate further

Explore

◎ Jenny investigates the sum of the cubes of the first two integers
She notices that the sum gives a square number:
$$1^3 + 2^3 = 9 \ (= 3^2)$$

◎ Jenny now investigates the sum of the cubes of the first three integers
She notices, again, that the sum gives a square number:
$$1^3 + 2^3 + 3^3 = 36 \ (= 6^2)$$

◎ Investigate the sum of the cubes of the first four integers

Investigate further

Explore

◎   One grain of rice is placed on the first square of a chessboard

◎   Two grains of rice are placed on the second square of a chessboard

◎   Four grains of rice are placed on the third square of a chessboard

◎   Eight grains of rice are placed on the fourth square of a chessboard etc

How many grains of rice will there be on the fifth square?

How many grains of rice will there be altogether on the first five squares?

How many grains of rice will there be on the tenth square?

How many grains of rice will there be altogether on the first ten squares?

Investigate further

Learn 2   Standard form

Examples:

a Convert these standard form numbers into ordinary form.
   i 2×10^2
   ii 6.82×10^5
   iii 3.001×10^3

b Convert these standard form numbers into ordinary form.
   i 2×10^{-2}
   ii 6.82×10^{-5}
   iii 3.001×10^{-3}

Standard form numbers are always written as:

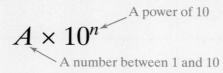

A power of 10

$$A \times 10^n$$

A number between 1 and 10

a i 2×10^2
        $= 2 \times 100$
        $= 200$

   ii 6.82×10^5
        $= 6.82 \times 100\,000$
        $= 682\,000$

   iii 3.001×10^3
        $= 3.001 \times 1000$
        $= 3001$

$$10^1 = 10$$
$$10^2 = 10 \times 10 = 100$$
$$10^3 = 10 \times 10 \times 10 = 1000$$
$$10^4 = 10 \times 10 \times 10 \times 10 = 10\,000$$
$$10^5 = 10 \times 10 \times 10 \times 10 \times 10 = 100\,000$$

b i 2×10^{-2}
$= 2 \times 0.01$
$= 0.02$

ii 6.82×10^{-5}
$= 6.82 \times 0.00001$
$= 0.0000682$

iii 3.001×10^{-3}
$= 3.001 \times 0.001$
$= 0.003001$

$$10^{-1} = \frac{1}{10^1} = \frac{1}{10} = 0.1$$
$$10^{-2} = \frac{1}{10^2} = \frac{1}{100} = 0.01$$
$$10^{-3} = \frac{1}{10^3} = \frac{1}{1000} = 0.001$$
$$10^{-4} = \frac{1}{10^4} = \frac{1}{10\ 000} = 0.0001$$
$$10^{-5} = \frac{1}{10^5} = \frac{1}{100\ 000} = 0.00001$$

Remember that multiplying by 10^{-1} is the same as dividing by 10^1, and multiplying by 10^{-2} is the same as dividing by 10^2, etc

c Write the following in standard form. Write your number in the form $A \times 10^n$ where A is a number between 1 and 10

i 65 000
$A = 6.5$, so $65\ 000 = 6.5 \times 10\ 000 = 6.5 \times 10^4$

ii 0.000000572
$A = 5.72$, so $0.000000572 = 5.72 \times 0.0000001 = 6.5 \times 10^{-7}$

Writing	Reading
Input the number 3.2×10^7 as 3.2 [EXP] 7 or 3.2 [EE] 7	On some calculators, the display 3.2ᵒ⁷ or 3.2 07 should be interpreted as 3.2×10^7

Apply 2

1 Write these numbers in standard form.

  a 3700

  b 23 000 000

  c 200 200

  d 8 500 000 000

  e 35

  f 0.005

  g 0.13

  h 0.000000178

  i 0.00000000002

  j 0.5

2 Write these standard form numbers as ordinary numbers.

  a 7×10^3

  b 7.6×10^5

  c 4.2×10^4

  d 6.085×10^2

  e 7.6635×10^1

  f 5.1×10^8

  g 3×10^{-1}

  h 1.25×10^{-3}

  i 3.086×10^{-4}

  j 6.6×10^{-10}

3 Get Real!
The distance from the Earth to the Moon is approximately 384 000 000 m. Write this number in standard form.

4 Get Real!

The mass of an electron is approximately
0.000000000000000000000000000000910939 kilograms (there are 30 zeros).
Write this number in standard form.

5 Get Real!

The table shows the diameters of the planets of the solar system.

Planet	Diameter (km)
Mercury	4.9×10^3
Venus	1.2×10^4
Earth	1.3×10^4
Mars	6.8×10^3
Jupiter	1.4×10^5
Saturn	1.2×10^5
Uranus	5.2×10^4
Neptune	4.9×10^4
Pluto	2.3×10^3

Place the planets in order of size, starting with the smallest.

6 Write the number 60^3 in standard form.

7 Calculate the following, giving your answers in standard form.

a $(4 \times 10^4) \times (2 \times 10^7)$

b $(5 \times 10^5) \times (3 \times 10^9)$

c $(5 \times 10^{-4})^2$

d $\dfrac{2.2 \times 10^1}{5.5 \times 10^{-6}}$

e $(3.3 \times 10^6) \times (3 \times 10^4)$

f $(2.5 \times 10^8) \times (5 \times 10^{-3})$

g $(4.5 \times 10^5) \times (2 \times 10^{11})$

h $\dfrac{4 \times 10^4}{2 \times 10^3}$

i $(1.5 \times 10^7)^2$

j $(2.2 \times 10^6) \div (4.4 \times 10^4)$

k $\dfrac{3.9 \times 10^5}{1.3 \times 10^8}$

8 Use your calculator to work out the following. Give your answers in standard form.

a $(3 \times 10^5) \times (3 \times 10^7)$

b $(5 \times 10^{-4})^2$

c $1 \div (2.5 \times 10^8)$

d $(4.55 \times 10^5) \times (6.2 \times 10^7)$

e $\dfrac{8 \times 10^{11}}{4 \times 10^3}$

f $(1.5 \times 10^7)^2$

g $(5 \times 10^5) + (3 \times 10^6)$

h $(2.4 \times 10^5) \times (3.5 \times 10^7)$

i $\dfrac{3.9 \times 10^8}{1.3 \times 10^{-5}}$

j $(8 \times 10^2) + (8 \times 10^4)$

k $(5 \times 10^5) \times (3.2 \times 10^9)$

l $(2.2 \times 10^2) \div (3.5 \times 10^{11})$

m $(5.2 \times 10^4) - (5.2 \times 10^3)$

n $(1.1 \times 10^3) - (1.11 \times 10^4)$

9 Get Real!

Some large numbers are:

> One million = 10^6
> One billion = 10^9
> One trillion = 10^{12}

a Write the number one billion in ordinary form.

b Write the number 50 million in standard form.

c How many millions are there in one trillion?

d Multiply three billion by four trillion. Give your answer in standard form.

10 A rectangle has length 1.4×10^4 metres and width 2.2×10^3 metres.
Calculate the area and perimeter of the rectangle.
Give your answers in standard form.

1.4×10^4 m

2.2×10^3 m

11 Alan says that $(4 \times 10^4) + (2 \times 10^4) = (6 \times 10^4)$.
Brian says that $(4 \times 10^4) + (2 \times 10^4) = (6 \times 10^8)$.
Who is correct?
Give a reason for your answer.

 **12** Given that $p = 4 \times 10^2$ and $q = 2 \times 10^{-1}$, calculate:

a $p \times q$ **b** $p \div q$ **c** $p + q$ **d** $p - q$ **e** p^2

13 Get Real!

The distance to the edge of the observable universe is approximately
4.6×10^{26} metres.
Express this distance in kilometres, giving your answer in standard form.

14 Get Real!

Anil saves some images onto a memory stick. Each image requires
32 000 bytes of memory. How many images can he save if the memory
stick has a memory of 1.36×10^8 bytes?
Give your answer in standard form.

15 Get Real!

The speed of light is approximately 3.0×10^8 m/s.
How far will light travel in one week?
Give your answer in standard form.

Explore

◎   A **googol** is the number 10^{100}, that is, one followed by one hundred zeros

◎   What can you find out about the googol?

(Investigate further)

Indices and standard form

ASSESS

The following exercise tests your understanding of this chapter,
with the questions appearing in order of increasing difficulty.

1 a Sam says numbers have two square roots.
George says some numbers have no square roots.
Who is right? Give a reason for your answer.

b Amelia joins in the conversation and says that all numbers have two
cube roots.
Is she right? Give a reason for your answer.

2 a Work out the following, giving your answers in index form.

   i $4^6 \times 4^2$ **v** $6^4 \times 6^2 \times 6^3$ **ix** $5^8 \div 5^7$

   ii $11^5 \times 11^3$ **vi** $10^4 \div 10^2$ **x** $2^3 \div 2^3$

   iii $(5^3)^2$ **vii** $21^7 \div 21^5$

   iv $7^5 \times 7$ **viii** $16^{10} \div 16^9$

b Find the value of:

   i $3^2 \times 4^2$ **ii** $3^4 \div 5^2$ **iii** $6^5 \times 6^3 \div 6^4$ **iv** $\dfrac{(10^8 \times 10^7)}{(10^7 \times 10^6)}$

c Which is larger:

   i 3^5 or 5^3 **ii** 11^2 or 2^{11} **iii** 2^4 or 4^2?

3 a The areas, in square kilometres, of some oceans and seas are shown below. Write them in increasing order of size and convert them to ordinary numbers.

   Arctic Ocean: $1.4 \times 10^7 \text{ km}^2$

   Atlantic Ocean: $8.24 \times 10^7 \text{ km}^2$

   Pacific Ocean: $1.65 \times 10^8 \text{ km}^2$

   Mediterranean Sea: $2.50 \times 10^6 \text{ km}^2$

   Gulf of Mexico: $1.54 \times 10^6 \text{ km}^2$

b Which is bigger: 1.1×10^8 or 99 999 999?

c Find the value of n in each of these.

   i $3.5 \times 10^n = 350\,000$ **ii** $5.69 \times 10^n = 56.9$ **iii** $4.006 \times 10^n = 400\,600$

4 a Write these numbers in standard form.

   i 0.003   **ii** 0.00000655   **iii** 0.1

b Write these standard form numbers as ordinary numbers.

   i 1×10^{-9} **ii** 4.22×10^{-6} **iii** 3.9958×10^{-5}

c Calculate the value of $3.52 \times 10^4 \times 2.2 \times 10^{-3}$.

d Calculate the value of $3.52 \times 10^4 \div 2.2 \times 10^{-3}$.

e A company employs 4.7×10^3 workers and the workers use, on average, 2.3×10^2 litres of water per year.
How many litres of water does the company use in a year?

f The mass of a hydrogen atom is 1.7×10^{-24} g.
One litre of air contains 2.5×10^{22} atoms of hydrogen.
What is the mass of the hydrogen atoms in one litre of air?

5 Find the values of the following, leaving your answers as fractions where appropriate.

   i 5^{-1} **iii** $12^3 \div 12^4$ **v** $2^6 \div 2^8$ **vii** $(\frac{1}{2})^{-3}$ **ix** $27^{\frac{2}{3}}$

   ii 23^0 **iv** 3^{-2} **vi** $(\frac{1}{4})^0$ **viii** $8^{\frac{1}{3}}$ **x** $16^{-\frac{3}{4}}$

7 Percentages

OBJECTIVES

D ▶ **Examiners would normally expect students who get a D grade to be able to:**

Increase or decrease a quantity by a given percentage

Express one quantity as a percentage of another

C ▶ **Examiners would normally expect students who get a C grade also to be able to:**

Work out a percentage increase or decrease

B ▶ **Examiners would normally expect students who get a B grade also to be able to:**

Understand how to use successive percentages

Work out compound interest

Work out reverse percentage problems

What you should already know ...

- Place values in decimals and putting decimals in order of size
- How to express fractions in their lowest terms (or simplest form)

- How to change between fractions, decimals and percentages
- Work out a percentage of a given quantity

VOCABULARY

Percentage – a number of parts per hundred, for example, 15% means $\frac{15}{100}$

Numerator – the number on the top of a fraction

Numerator ⟶ $\frac{3}{8}$ ⟵ Denominator

Denominator – the number on the bottom of a fraction

Multiplier – a number used to multiply an amount

Interest – money paid to you by a bank, building society or other financial institution if you put your money in an account or the money you pay for borrowing from a bank

Simple interest – pays interest only on the sum of money originally invested

Compound interest – pays interest on both the original sum and the interest already earned

Principal – the money put into the bank or borrowed from the bank

Rate – the percentage at which interest is added, usually expressed as per cent per annum (year)

Time – usually measured in years for the purpose of working out interest

Amount – the total you will have in the bank or the total you will owe the bank, at the end of the period of time

Balance – the amount of money you have in your bank account or the amount of money you owe after you have paid a deposit

Deposit – an amount of money you pay towards the cost of an item, with the rest of the cost to be paid later

Discount – a reduction in the price, perhaps for paying in cash or paying early

VAT (Value Added Tax) – a tax that has to be added on to the price of goods or services

Depreciation – a reduction in value, for example, due to age or condition

Credit – when you buy goods 'on credit' you do not pay all the cost at once; instead you make a number of payments at regular intervals, often once a month

Learn 1   Increasing or decreasing by a given percentage

Examples:

a Parveen's bus fare to town is 80p. The bus fares go up by 5%. How much is the new fare?

10% of 80p = 8p 5% of 80p = 4p New fare = 84p	Original fare = 100% New fare = (100 + 5)% = 105% = 1.05 New fare = 1.05 × 80p = 84p

b Find the new price of a £350 TV after a 4% reduction.

1% of £350 = £3.50 4% of £350 = £3.50 × 4 = £14 New price = £350 − £14 = £336	Original price = 100% New price = (100 − 4)% = 96% = 0.96 New price = 0.96 × £350 = £336

Apply 1

1 Increase 25 cm by 10%.

2 Decrease 700 g by 5%.

3 Decrease £450 by 20%.

4 Increase £3 by 8%.

5 Get Real!
Todd is paid £300 per week.
He gets a 4% pay rise.
What is his new weekly pay?

6 Get Real!

A package holiday is priced at £660.
Gary gets a 10% discount for booking before the end of January.
How much does he pay?

7 Get Real!

Emma gets a 15% discount on purchases from Aqamart.
How much does she pay for a TV priced at £500?

8 Get Real!

A music centre costs £280.
VAT at $17\frac{1}{2}$% has to be added to the bill.
What is the total cost of the music centre?

9 Get Real!

Jared buys a jacket in a sale.
The price ticket says £70.
There is a label on the rack saying 'Take 25% off all marked prices'.
How much will Jared pay for the jacket?

10 Increase 125 cm by 16%.

11 Increase 340 g by 9%.

12 Decrease £560 by 22%.

13 Decrease £9.55 by 12%.

14 Get Real!

The population of Baytown was 65 970 in 1990.
By the year 2000, Baytown's population had gone up by 27%.
What was the population in 2000?

15 Get Real!

Becky buys a new car for £12 499.
Over 2 years, it depreciates by 45%.
What is the value of the car after 2 years?

16 Get Real!

A garden shed is for sale at '£550 + VAT'.
If VAT is $17\frac{1}{2}$%, what is the total cost of the shed?

17 Get Real!

The bill for a repair is £57.35
VAT at $17\frac{1}{2}$% has to be added to the bill.
What is the total cost of the repair?

18 Paul needs to increase 45 kg by 5%.
He writes down 45 × 1.5 = 67.5 kg.
Is he correct?
Give a reason for your answer.

Explore

- ⊚ Jo wants to buy a music centre priced at £650
- ⊚ She has to put down £100 as a deposit
- ⊚ There are two ways she can pay the rest of the price (the balance)
  1 The EasyPay Option:
    - 14% credit charge on the balance
    - 12 equal monthly payments
  2 The PayLess Option:
    - 3% added each month to the amount owing at the beginning of the month
    - pay £50 per month until the balance is paid off

  (Note: in the last month Jo will only pay the remaining balance, not a full £50)

- ⊚ Using a calculator, investigate these two options to advise Jo which one is best
- ⊚ Would your advice be different if EasyPay charged 11% or PayLess charged $3\frac{1}{2}$% each month?

Investigate further

Learn 2 Using successive percentage changes

Examples: **a** There are 200 fish in a pond. 75% of them are goldfish.
36% of these goldfish are less than 6 cm long.
How many fish in the pond are goldfish and less than 6 cm long?

First find 75% of 200:   50% of 200 = 100
                              25% of 200 =   50
                              75% of 200 = 150 fish are goldfish

Then find 36% of 150:   36% of 100 = 36
                              36% of   50 = 18
                              36% of 150 = 54 goldfish are less than 6 cm long

For successive percentages, work out the first percentage and use your answer to work out the second percentage (usually the best method if you are not allowed to use a calculator)

 b Paul buys a car for £25 000. It depreciates by 35% in the first year and 20% in the second year. What is it worth after two years?

The original price is 100%
In the first year, it becomes (100 − 35)% which is 65%
    £25 000 × 0.65 = £16 250   ← *The new 100%*

At the start of the second year, the price is £16 250
This becomes (100 − 20)% which is 80%
    £16 250 × 0.80 = £13 000

After two years it is worth £13 000   *Using multipliers this can be worked out on a calculator as:*
                                                £25 000 × 0.65 × 0.80 = £13 000

Apply 2

1 There are 800 students at Uptown College. 20% of them have a driving licence. 35% of those with driving licences drive to college. How many students drive to college?

2 In London, 250 teachers attend a meeting.
60% of them are women.
18% of these women are under 30 years old.
How many of the women are under 30?

3 Kate earns £900 per month. On average, she spends 25% of this at the supermarket. 60% of her supermarket spending is on food. How much does Kate spend on food each month?

4 Jack bought shares worth £4000 in January 2002. By January 2003, the value of his shares had risen by 15%. Between January 2003 and January 2004, their value rose by 5%. What was the value of the shares in January 2004?

5 Alice is answering question **4** above. She writes:
  15% + 5% equals 20%
  20% is the same as one fifth
  One fifth of £4000 is £800
What mistake has Alice made?

6 Ellie was paid £8.00 per hour in 2003. In 2004, she got a pay rise of 5%, and in 2005, her pay rise was $2\frac{1}{2}\%$. How much was Ellie paid at the end of 2005?

7 Which of these is bigger:

a a 25% increase followed by a 10% decrease

b a 10% decrease followed by a 25% increase?

8 Assad says that a decrease of 20% followed by a decrease of 10% is the same as a decrease of 30%. Is Assad correct? Give a reason for your answer.

9 The population of Mellowby village is 1250.
44% of them are pensioners.
26% of the pensioners live alone.
How many pensioners live alone in Mellowby?

10 There were 160 people at a concert.
55% of them bought a programme.
$12\frac{1}{2}\%$ of these programmes were left behind after the concert.
How many programmes were left behind?

11 Marie bought a painting for £750. In the first year, the value of the painting went up by 16% and in the second year it went down by 35%. Find the value of the painting after two years.

12 Brad bought shares worth £15 000 in April 2001. By April 2002, the value of his shares had dropped by 8.2%. In the following year, the value of the shares dropped by 11.5%.
What were Brad's shares worth in April 2003?

13 A puppy weighed 3.2 kg at 8 weeks old. His weight went up by 6% in the next week and by 7% in the following week.
What did he weigh when he was 10 weeks old?

Explore

 Jack's beanstalk grows 35% each month

 In January it is 12 m high

 How many months does it take to reach 50 m?

 When does it reach 100 m?

> Investigate further

Learn 3 Compound interest

Examples:

a Find the compound interest on £3000 invested for 2 years at 5% per annum.

	Principal	Interest
Year 1	£3000	5% of £3000 = $\frac{5}{100}$ × £3000 = 150
Year 2	£3000 + £150 = £3150	5% of £3150 = $\frac{5}{100}$ × £3150 = 157.5 ← This is £157.50

Total interest = £150 + £157.50 = £307.50

b Find the compound interest on £8000 invested for 3 years at 4.6% per annum.

The compound interest formula is:

$$\text{Amount} = \text{Principal} \times \left[1 + \frac{\text{Rate}}{100}\right]^n \quad \text{where } n \text{ is the number of years}$$

	Principal	Interest by 4.6%
Year 1	£8000	£8000 × 1.046 = £8368
Year 2	£8368	£8368 × 1.046 = £8752.928
Year 3	£8752.928	£8752.928 × 1.046 = £9155.5627

Amount = £9155.56
Interest = £9155.56 − £8000 = £1155.56

This has to be rounded to £9155.56

In this example, successive principals were multiplied by 1.046 so the final amount = £8000 × 1.046 × 1.046 × 1.046 or £8000 × 1.046^3 = £9155.5627

Apply 3

1 Find the compound interest on £500 invested for 2 years at 4% per annum.

2 Find the compound interest on £2000 invested for 2 years at 7% per annum.

3 £4000 is invested at 3% per annum compound interest.
Find the amount at the end of 2 years.

4 £1000 is invested at 10% per annum compound interest.
Find the amount at the end of 3 years.

5 Get Real!
The value of machinery in a factory depreciates by 20% each year.
The machinery was bought for £74 500.
What was its value after 2 years?

6 Find the compound interest on £5850 invested for 3 years at 3.4% per annum.

7 Find the compound interest on £2000 invested for 5 years at $7\frac{1}{2}$% per annum.

8 £14 000 is invested at $9\frac{1}{4}$% per annum compound interest.
Find the amount at the end of 6 years.

9 Jo borrows £4500 for 3 years at 3% per annum simple interest. Kevin borrows the same amount at 3% per annum compound interest.
How much more does Kevin have to pay back?

10 Get Real!
Liam has inherited some money from his grandmother.
He wants to invest it for 5 years.
He could put it in AqaBank or in SmartMoney.
AqaBank pays 5.27% per annum simple interest.
SmartMoney pays 4.81% per annum compound interest.
Where should Liam invest his inheritance to earn the most interest?

11 £6000 is invested at $4\frac{3}{4}$% per annum compound interest.
After how many years will this amount to more than £7000?

12 Get Real!
A bird colony is decreasing at 16% per annum.
If the original population was 600 birds, after how many years will there be fewer than 200 birds left?

Learn 4 Expressing one quantity as a percentage of another and finding a percentage increase or decrease

Examples:

a Express 84p as a percentage of £20.

Make sure both quantities are in the **same units**
Write them as a fraction and multiply by 100 to change to a percentage

Working in pounds,
change 84p to £0.84

0.84 as a fraction of 20 is $\frac{0.84}{20}$

To convert a fraction to a
percentage you multiply by 100:

$$\frac{0.84}{20} = \frac{0.84}{20} \times 100\%$$

$$= \frac{0.84}{20_1} \times \cancel{100}^5\%$$

$$= 4.2\%$$

Working in pence,
change £20 to 2000p

84 as a fraction of 2000 is $\frac{84}{2000}$

To convert a fraction to a
percentage you multiply by 100:

$$\frac{84}{2000} = \frac{84}{2000} \times 100\%$$

$$= \frac{\cancel{84}^{42}}{\cancel{2000}_{\cancel{1000}_{10}}} \times \cancel{100}^1\%$$

$$= 4.2\%$$

b Find the percentage increase when the temperature goes up from 20°C to 26°C.

Temperature increase = 6°
6 as a fraction of 20 is $\frac{6}{20}$
To convert a fraction to a percentage you multiply by 100:

$$\frac{6}{20} = \frac{6}{20} \times 100\%$$

$$= \frac{6}{20_1} \times \cancel{100}^5\%$$

$$= 30\% \text{ increase}$$

Make sure both quantities are in the **same units**

Write this as a fraction and multiply by 100 to change to a percentage **(The original quantity has to be on the bottom of the fraction)**

c Find the percentage decrease when the price of a toy falls from £12.50 to £11.75

Price decrease = £0.75
£0.75 as a fraction of £12.50 is $\frac{0.75}{12.50}$
To convert a fraction to a percentage you multiply by 100:

$$\frac{0.75}{12.50} = \frac{0.75}{12.50} \times 100\%$$

$$= \frac{0.75}{\cancel{12.50}_{\cancel{25}_1}} \times \cancel{100}^{\cancel{200}^8}\%$$

$$= 6\% \text{ decrease}$$

Apply 4

1 Express 12p as a percentage of 16p.

2 Express 20 kg as a percentage of 50 kg.

3 Express 85 mm as a percentage of 10 cm.

4 Express 42p as a percentage of £7.

5 Express 385 g as a percentage of 35 kg.

6 **Get Real!**
There are 800 students in Uptown College.
96 of these students walk to college each day.
What percentage of the students walk to college?

7 **Get Real!**
Chris has 50 books on his shelves.
29 of these books are science fiction.
What percentage of his books are science fiction?

8 **Get Real!**
The price of a packet of biscuits goes up from 30p to 36p.
Find the percentage increase.

9 **Get Real!**
Becky's curtains were 60 cm long before she washed them.
After the wash they were only 51 cm long.
Find the percentage decrease in length.

10 **Get Real!**
Sam buys a guitar for £125 and sells it for £160.
Find his percentage profit.

11 Express 7 cm as a percentage of 12 cm.

12 Express £17.64 as a percentage of £72.

13 Express 65 g as a percentage of 5 kg.

14 Express 90 cm as a percentage of 8 m.

15 Express 38p as a percentage of £12.

16 Anna's answer to question **10** is 21.9%.
What mistake has she made?

17 **Get Real!**
Mel wanted to buy a sofa priced at £1450.
The salesman asked for a deposit of £348.
What percentage of the price was this?

 **18 Get Real!**

Out of 3600 claims on household insurance, 522 were for broken windows.
What percentage of claims were for broken windows?

19 Grace has £6.50 in her purse.
She puts 50p in a charity box.
What percentage of her money has gone to charity?

 **20 Get Real!**

The value of a house goes down from £166 000 to £141 100.
Find the percentage decrease.

21 Get Real!

A landlord puts the rent on a flat up from £280 per month to £301
per month.
Find the percentage increase.

22 Get Real!

Jo buys a painting for £975 and sells it a year later for £700.
Find her percentage loss.

Learn 5 Reverse percentage problems

Examples:

a A pair of jeans are priced at £35 in a sale. They have been reduced by 30%.
What was their original price?

Work out what percentage the new price is of the original price.
Divide by this value to find 1%.
Multiply by 100 to find 100%. ⟵ 100% − 30%

70% of the original price = £35
1% of the original price = £35 ÷ 70 = £0.50
100% of the original price = £0.50 × 100 = £50

b The cost of a holiday has gone up by 15%. It is now £483.
What was the price before the increase?
Using the method above: ⟵ 100% + 15%

115% of the original price = £483
1% of the original price = £483 ÷ 115 = £4.20
100% of the original price = £4.20 × 100 = £420

Apply 5

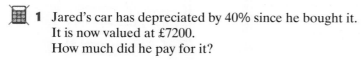

1 Jared's car has depreciated by 40% since he bought it.
It is now valued at £7200.
How much did he pay for it?

2 The cost of Suzi's car insurance has gone up by 10% this year.
She now pays £473.
What did she pay last year?

3 Household goods have been reduced by 25% in a sale.
A washing machine is now priced at £465.
What was the price of the washing machine before the sale?

4 Dean bought a guitar in a sale for £54.
He knew it had been reduced by 10%.
Dean said 'I saved £5.40 by getting the guitar in the sale.'
Explain why Dean is wrong.

5 The train fare from Ansaville to Bisterton has gone up by 8%.
It is now £8.10
What was the fare before the increase?

6 The number of patients on a doctor's register has increased to 2055.
This is an increase of 37% over 5 years.
How many patients were on the register 5 years ago?

7 Chris took out a loan from a finance company.
He had to pay it back with interest after one year.
The finance company charged interest at 28% per annum.
Chris paid back £4480. How much was the original loan?

8 The machinery in a factory is valued at £765 000.
Depreciation was 18% over the past year.
What was the value of the machinery a year ago?

9 A motorist is charged £246.44 to have her car serviced.
This charge includes VAT at $17\frac{1}{2}$%.
What was the charge before the VAT was added?

10 A computer is priced at £795, which includes VAT at $17\frac{1}{2}$%.
The computer is bought by a charity, who can reclaim the VAT.
How much can the charity reclaim?

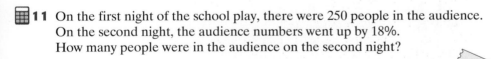

HINT Some of the last four questions will require
reverse percentages and some will not.

11 On the first night of the school play, there were 250 people in the audience.
On the second night, the audience numbers went up by 18%.
How many people were in the audience on the second night?

12 The price of admission to the cinema has gone up by 25%.
Tim pays £4.80 for his ticket.
Andy says the old price must have been £3.60
Explain why Andy is wrong.

13 A house in Upville was valued at £255 000 in January 2005.
Over the next year, houses in Upville depreciated by 12%.
What was the value of the house in January 2006?

14 The number of employees in a factory went up by 22%.
The factory now employs 366 people.
How many were there before the increase?

Percentages

The following exercise tests your understanding of this chapter, with the questions appearing in order of increasing difficulty.

1 a Write 60p as a percentage of £1.20

   b What is 150 cm as a percentage of 3 km?

   c David has bought Victoria an 18 carat gold bracelet.
Pure gold is 24 carat.
What percentage of Victoria's bracelet is gold?

   d A bag of sand is labelled as 50 kg.
It actually contains 2.5% more.
How much sand does it contain?

   e Ms Berry has picked 1.2 kg of blackberries for making jam.
She needs 15% more to make her recipe.
What weight of blackberries does the recipe require?

2 a A book is designed to have 650 pages.
When the author finished the manuscript he found he had written 754 pages.
What percentage increase is this?

   b A box of 144 pens is bought for £10 and individual pens are sold at 10p each.
What is the percentage profit?

   c Toad of Toad Hall bought his latest car for £18 000.
A week later he crashed it and, after repair, sold it for £11 700.
What was his percentage loss?

   d 100 apples are bought for £17 but 5% are found to be damaged and not saleable. The rest are sold at 20p each.
What is the percentage profit?

   e Pythagoras makes a calculator error while using his famous theorem!
He wants to find the value of $\sqrt{112}$ but instead finds $\sqrt{121}$.
What is the percentage error in his calculation?

3 a The population in a village of 3600 people grows by 7% per year.
What is the population after:

     i 1 year   **ii** 2 years?

   b A firm employs 6500 workers.
The work force depreciates by 14% each year.
How many workers are there after:

     i 1 year   **ii** 2 years?

   c Use the compound interest formula to find the interest on £25 000 at 4% over 5 years.

   d Farmer Barleymow has sold 20% of his land to a builder.
He now owns 60 acres of land.
How much land did Farmer Barleymow originally own?

   e After a discount of 12%, a kitchen is priced at £4224.
What was the price before the discount?

   f Mr Moneybags invests a sum of money in a dubious share venture.
The investment initially increases by 10% but then decreases by 16% to £23 100.
How much was his original investment?

8 Ratio and proportion

OBJECTIVES

D **Examiners would normally expect students who get a D grade to be able to:**

Solve simple ratio and proportion problems, such as finding the ratio of teachers to students in a school

C **Examiners would normally expect students who get a C grade also to be able to:**

Solve more complex ratio and proportion problems, such as sharing out money between two groups in the ratio of their numbers

Solve ratio and proportion problems using the unitary method

B **Examiners would normally expect students who get a B grade also to be able to:**

Calculate proportional changes using a multiplier

A **Examiners would normally expect students who get an A grade also to be able to:**

Solve direct and inverse proportion problems

Interpret graphs of direct and inverse proportion relationships

What you should already know ...

- How to add, subtract, multiply and divide numbers

- How to simplify fractions

VOCABULARY

Constant – a number that does not change, for example, the formula $P = 4l$ states that the perimeter of a square is always four times the length of one side; 4 is a constant and P and l are variables

Ratio – the ratio of two or more numbers or quantities is a way of comparing their sizes, for example, if a school has 25 teachers and 500 students, the ratio of teachers to students is 25 to 500, or 25 : 500 (read as 25 to 500)

Unitary ratio – a ratio in the form $1 : n$ or $n : 1$; for example, for every 100 female babies born, 105 male babies are born. The ratio of the number of females to the number of males is 100 : 105; as a unitary ratio, this is 1 : 1.05, which means that, for every female born, 1.05 males are born

Proportion – if a class has 12 boys and 18 girls, the proportion of boys in the class is $\frac{12}{30}$, which simplifies to $\frac{2}{5}$, and the proportion of girls is $\frac{18}{30}$, which simplifies to $\frac{3}{5}$ (the **ratio** of boys to girls is 12 : 18, which simplifies to 2 : 3) – a proportion compares one part with the whole; a ratio compares parts with one another

Unitary method – a way of calculating quantities that are in proportion, for example, if 6 items cost £30 and you want to know the cost of 10 items, you can first find the cost of one item by dividing by 6, then find the cost of 10 by multiplying by 10

6 items cost £30

1 item costs $\dfrac{£30}{6}$ = £5

10 items cost $10 \times £5$ = £50

Direct proportion – if two variables are in direct proportion, one is equal to a constant multiple of the other, so that if one increases, the other increases and if one decreases then the other decreases

In general $x \propto y$ and $x = kx$

Inverse proportion – if two variables are in inverse proportion, their product is a constant; so that if one increases, the other decreases and vice versa

In general $x \propto \frac{1}{y}$ and $x = k\frac{1}{y}$ and $xy = k$

Learn 1   Finding and simplifying ratios

Examples:

a A school has 50 teachers and 900 students.
Write down the teacher : student ratio and express it in its simplest form.

First write the numbers in the correct order for the ratio and separate them with a colon symbol.

The colon symbol is used to express ratio

The teacher : student ratio is 50 : 900.

'50 : 900' is read as 'fifty to nine hundred'

Like cancelling a fraction, the ratio can be simplified.

Both numbers have been divided by 10

Ratio = 50 : 900 = 5 : 90 = 1 : 18

Both numbers have been divided by 5

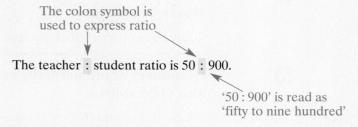

This is like simplifying fractions

The ratio in its simplest form is 1 : 18.

This means that, for every teacher in this school, there are 18 students (or the number of teachers is $\frac{1}{18}$ of the number of students).

b A shopkeeper buys boxes of chocolates for £3.50 and sells them for £4.25
What is the ratio of the profit to the cost price?

The profit is the selling price minus the cost price = £4.25 − £3.50 = 75p.

Ratio of profit to cost price = 75p : £3.50

Make sure the amounts are both in pence or both in pounds. Using pence is probably easier

Divide both numbers by 5

= 75p : 350p

= 75 : 350 ← The ratio 75p to 350p is the same ratio as 75 to 350

= 15 : 70 ← Divide both numbers by 5 again, then the ratio cannot be simplified any more

= 3 : 14

$$\frac{75}{350} \overset{\div 5}{\underset{\div 5}{=}} \frac{15}{70} \overset{\div 5}{\underset{\div 5}{=}} \frac{3}{14}$$

Compare with the fraction simplification

The ratio of 3 to 14 means that the shopkeeper makes a profit of £3 for every £14 she spends on boxes of chocolates (if she sells them all).

It also means that:

• the profit is $\frac{3}{17}$ of the selling price
• the cost price is $\frac{14}{17}$ of the selling price.

Check that you can see where the numerators and denominators have come from.

Also check that $\frac{3}{17}$ of £4.25 is 75p and $\frac{14}{17}$ of £4.25 is £3.50

Apply 1

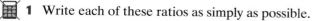

1 Write each of these ratios as simply as possible.

a 2 : 4   **e** 2 : 12   **i** 24 : 36   **m** 0.3 : 0.8

b 2 : 6   **f** 2 : 14   **j** 25 : 100   **n** $2\frac{1}{2} : 7\frac{1}{2}$

c 2 : 8   **g** 12 : 36   **k** $\frac{2}{3} : \frac{4}{9}$ **o** 20% : 80%

d 2 : 10   **h** 18 : 24   **l** 1.5 : 2.5   **p** 25 : 200

2 a Write down three different pairs of numbers that are in the ratio 1 : 2.

b Write down three different pairs of numbers that are in the ratio 1 : 4.

c Explain how to find pairs of numbers that are in the ratio 1 : 4.

d Pippa writes the three pairs of numbers 6 and 9, 9 and 12, and 12 and 15. She says these pairs of numbers are all in the same ratio. What has Pippa done wrong?

3 Get Real!

A recipe for pastry needs 50 grams of butter and 100 grams of flour.

a What is the ratio of butter to flour? What is the ratio of flour to butter?

b How much butter is needed for 200 grams of flour?

c How much flour is needed for 30 grams of butter?

d What fraction is the butter's weight of the flour's weight?

4 Get Real!

On a music download site, a track costs 75p and an album costs £7.50
Find the ratio of the cost of a track to the cost of an album, A, in its
simplest form.

5 Get Real!

A recipe for cheese sauce for four people needs these ingredients:

- 600 mℓ milk, warmed
- 100 g grated cheese
- 40 g flour
- 40 g butter
- seasoning

a List the ingredients needed to make enough cheese sauce for
two people.

b Explain how to find the quantities to make enough cheese sauce
for ten people.

6 Get Real!

a Find, in their simplest forms, the teacher : student ratios for these schools.

School	Number of teachers	Number of students
School 1	75	1500
School 2	15	240
School 3	22	374
School 4	120	1800
School 5	65	1365

The numbers have been made simple so
that it is easy for you to work them out
Real schools have harder numbers!

b i If a school with 50 teachers had the same teacher : student ratio as
School 1, how many students would it have?

ii If a school with 2000 students had the same teacher : student ratio
as School 1, how many teachers would it have?

c Which school has the 'best' teacher to student ratio? (That is,
which school has the smallest number of students for each teacher?)

 **7 Get Real!**

a Find the profit : cost price ratio for these items.

Item	Cost price	Selling price	Profit
Litre of petrol	85p		5p
Car	£4500	£5000	
Calculator	£15		£10
Book	£2.80	£3.50	
Magazine		£1.10	15p
Sandwich		£1.25	50p

b Use the profit : cost price ratio for the car to write fraction statements like those at the end of Learn **1**.

c In question **6**, all the ratios were in the form 1 : *something* (mathematically, 1 : *n*) so they were easy to compare.
How could you compare the ratios in part **a**? Would a calculator help?

8 Get Real!

a In a salsa class, the ratio of women to men is 5 : 4.
i There are 10 women in the class. How many men are there?
ii The number of women and the number of men both double. Does the ratio change? Explain your answer.

b In the jazz dance class, the ratio of men to women is 2 : 3 and there are 10 dancers altogether.
i How many men and how many women are there in the jazz dance class?
ii Two more men and two more women join the class. Does the ratio of men to women increase, decrease or stay the same? Explain your answer.

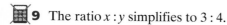 **9** The ratio $x : y$ simplifies to 3 : 4.

a If x is 6, what is y?   **c** If y is 2, what is x?

b If y is 12, what is x?   **d** If x and y add to 35, what are x and y?

10 Make up another question like question **9** and give the answers.

11 Here is a pattern sequence.

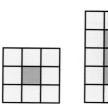 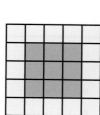 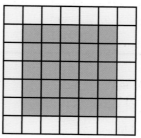

a Does the ratio 'number of green squares : number of yellow squares' increase, decrease or stay the same as the shapes get bigger?
Show how you worked out your answer.

b Draw your own sequence where the ratio of the number of green squares to the number of yellow squares stays the same as the shapes get bigger.

Explore

Map scales are often expressed in ratio form, such as 1 : 100 000

◎   Look at some maps (perhaps you can use examples from geography)

◎   How are the scales of the maps shown? Write down some examples

◎   Find out what a scale in the form 1 : 100 000 means

◎   Find out how to express map scales such as '2 cm to 1 km' in ratio form

◎   What distance in real life does 3 cm on a 1 : 100 000 map represent?

(Investigate further)

Learn 2   Using ratios to find quantities

Example:

In a school of 1000 students, the ratio of boys to girls is 9 : 11.
How many boys and how many girls are there in the school?

For this problem, you need to divide 1000 students in the ratio 9 : 11 to find the number of boys and the number of girls.

The ratio shows that *for every* 9 boys there are 11 girls. So *in every* 20 students, there are 9 boys and 11 girls, as 9 + 11 = 20.

Out of every 20 students,
9 are boys

Out of every 20 students,
11 are girls

The fraction of boys in the school is $\frac{9}{20}$ and the fraction of girls is $\frac{11}{20}$

The number of boys in the school is $\frac{9}{20}$ of 1000.

$$\frac{1}{20} \text{ of } 1000 = \frac{1000}{20} = 50$$

So $\frac{9}{20}$ of $1000 = 50 \times 9 = 450$

The number of girls in the school is $\frac{11}{20}$ of 1000, which is $11 \times 50 = 550$.

So the number of boys is 450 and the number of girls is 550.

Check that the number of boys and the number of girls add up to 1000, the total number of students in the school

Apply 2

1 Divide these numbers and quantities in the ratio 1 : 2.

    a 150   **c** £4.50   **e** £1.50

    b 300   **d** 6 litres   **f** 1.5 litres

2 Divide the numbers and quantities in question **1** in the ratio 2 : 3.

3 Divide the numbers and quantities in question **1** in the ratio 3 : 7.

4 Divide the numbers and quantities in question **1** in the ratio 1 : 3 : 6.

5 Get Real!

Pastry is made from fat and flour in the ratio 1 : 2.

a How much flour is needed to make 150 g of pastry?

b How much fat is needed to make 6 ounces of pastry?

c How much pastry can you make if you have plenty of flour but only 60 g of fat?

6 *You should be able to do the first four of these schools without a calculator but you will need one for School E and for parts **b** and **c**.*

a Find the number of boys and the number of girls in these schools.

School	Total number of students	Boy : girl ratio
School A	750	1 : 1
School B	900	4 : 5
School C	1800	4 : 5
School D	1326	6 : 7
School E	1184	301 : 291

School E shows the most realistic ratio. What is the boy : girl ratio in your school or college?

b Find the boy : girl ratios in part **a** in the form 1 : n (in other words, find how many girls there are for every boy).

c Which school has the largest proportion of boys? Give a reason for your answer.

7 This table shows the ratio of carbohydrate to fat to protein in some foods.

a Find the amount of fat in 150 g of each of the foods.

Food	Carbohydrate : fat : protein
Chicken sandwich	1 : 1 : 1
Grilled salmon	0 : 1 : 1
Yoghurt (whole milk)	1 : 2 : 1
Taco chips	10 : 4 : 1
Bread	7 : 2 : 1
Milk	2 : 3 : 2

HINT Use a calculator for milk as the ratios do not work out easily. Round your answers to the nearest 5 grams.

b Which of these foods would you avoid if you were on a low-fat diet?

c How many grams of yoghurt would you need to eat to have 100 g of protein?

d Which of these foods would you avoid if you were on a low-carbohydrate diet?

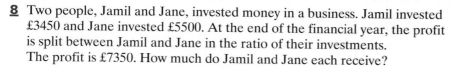

8 Two people, Jamil and Jane, invested money in a business. Jamil invested £3450 and Jane invested £5500. At the end of the financial year, the profit is split between Jamil and Jane in the ratio of their investments. The profit is £7350. How much do Jamil and Jane each receive?

9 Bronze for coins can be made of copper, tin and zinc in the ratio 95 : 4 : 1.

a How much of each metal is needed to make 1 kilogram of bronze?

b How much of each metal is needed to make 10 kilograms of bronze?

c How much of each metal is needed to make half a kilogram of bronze?

d How much zinc would there be in a coin weighing 6 grams?

Learn 3 Ratio and proportion

Example:

A teacher pays £27.60 for 6 calculators.
How much does he pay for 15 of the same calculators?

A useful method for finding quantities in proportion, or to solve 'best buy' problems, is the unitary method (shown below).

Write the statement with the number you want to change (the number of calculators) at the start

6 calculators cost £27.60

Next write the statement starting with 1

1 calculator costs $\dfrac{£27.60}{6} = £4.60$

Divide the cost of 6 calculators by 6 to find the cost of 1 calculator

When you know the cost of 1 calculator you can find the cost of any number

15 calculators cost 15 × £4.60 = £69

Multiply the cost of 1 calculator by 15 to find the cost of 15 calculators

Finally, write the statement starting with the number you want (15 in this case)

Check that the answer is reasonable
Do an estimate: the cost of 15 calculators is between 2 and 3 times the cost of 6 calculators

All the calculating can be left to the end if you prefer:

6 calculators cost £27.60

1 calculator costs $\dfrac{£27.60}{6}$

15 calculators cost $15 × \dfrac{£27.60}{6} = £69$

This is the same as
$\dfrac{£27.60}{6} × 1.5$ or $£27.60 × \frac{15}{6}$

If you feel confident with problems like this, you can do them in one step by combining the multiplication and division, but be careful and check that your answer is sensible

Apply 3

1 Get Real!
Check that, in the example above, the ratio 'cost of 1 calculator : cost of 6 calculators : cost of 15 calculators' is 1 : 6 : 15.

 2 Get Real!
Sajid worked for 8 hours and was paid £30.

  a How much will he be paid for working 10 hours at the same rate of pay?

  b Complete a copy of this table. Plot the values in the table as points on a graph, using the numbers of hours worked as the *x*-coordinates and the money earned as the corresponding *y*-coordinates.

Number of hours worked	0	2	4	6	8	10
Money earned (£)					30	

c The points should lie in a straight line through (0, 0).

  i Explain why.

  ii What does the gradient of the line represent?

  iii Show how to use the graph to find out how much Sajid earns in 5 hours.

3 Get Real!

50 grams of fish food will feed 8 fish for 1 day.

a How much food would 12 fish require for 1 day?

b How many days can 2 fish survive on 50 grams of food?

c How much food is needed for 10 fish for 7 days?

4 Get Real!

Lovelylocks shampoo is sold in travel size and large size.

	Amount of shampoo	Price
Travel size	40 grams	75p
Large size	125 grams	£2.25

Calculate which of the two sizes gives you better value for money. Show all your working clearly.

5 Get Real!

'Rich and Dark' chocolate is sold in a 55 g size costing 60p and a 100 g size costing £1.05. Which of these is better value for money?

6 Get Real!

On the motorway, Jacob drove a distance of 84 miles in 3 hours.

a How far would Jacob travel in 4 hours at the same average speed?

b How far would he go in three-quarters of an hour at this average speed?

c How long would it take for Jacob to travel 60 miles at this average speed?

7 Get Real!

Notice that the two parts of this question are really the same!
Use part **a** to help you work out part **b**.

a 80% of a number is 16. Use the unitary method to find 100% of the number.

b A sweater is reduced by 20% to £16 in the sale. What was the original price of the sweater?

8 a Two numbers are in the ratio 1 : 0.75
The first number is 12; what is the second?

b Two numbers are in the ratio 1 : 0.75
The second number is 12; what is the first?

c Three numbers are in the ratio 1.1 : 1 : 0.9
The third number is 36; what are the other two numbers?

9 Get Real!

The weights of objects on other planets are proportional to their weights on Earth. A person weighing 120 pounds on Earth would weigh 20 pounds on the moon and 300 pounds on Jupiter.

a What would a teenager weighing 80 pounds on Earth weigh on Jupiter?

b What would a rock weighing 10 kilograms on the moon weigh on Earth?

c This graph shows the weights of objects on Jupiter compared with their weights on Earth. Copy the graph and sketch a line on it to show the weights of objects on the moon compared with their weights on Earth.

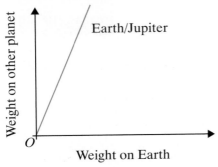

d Express the ratio 'weight of object on Earth : weight of object on moon : weight of object on Jupiter' in its simplest form.

Explore

You may already know something about the Fibonacci sequences

Each term is found by adding together the last two terms

So, starting with 1, 1, the series continues 1, 1, 2, 3, 5, 8, ...

◎ Carry the sequence on until you have at least 20 terms (would a spreadsheet be useful?)

◎ Work out, in the form $1 : n$, the ratio of
    term 1 to term 2
    term 2 to term 3
    term 3 to term 4 and so on

◎ What can you say about the ratios as you go through the series?

Investigate further

Learn 4   Calculating proportional changes

Examples: In a laboratory experiment, the number of bacteria in a colony increases by 10% every hour. At the start, the number of bacteria is 1000.

   a What is the number of bacteria after 1 hour?
   b What is the number of bacteria after 2 hours?
   c What is the number of bacteria after 10 hours?

> You could work out 10% of the number of bacteria and add it on but the one-step method here is more powerful
> 100% + 10% is 110%

   a After one hour, the number of bacteria = 110% of 1000 = $\frac{110}{100} \times 1000 = 1100$

> $\frac{110}{100} = 1.1$, so finding 110% of something is the same as multiplying it by 1.1

   b After 2 hours, the number of bacteria is 110% of 1100 = $1.1 \times 1100 = 1210$ and so on.

> You could do this step by step, multiplying the number each hour by 1.1 to get the number for the next hour, but it takes time! This method does all 10 multiplications in one step

   c After 10 hours, the number of bacteria is $1000 \times 1.1^{10} = 2593.74246... \approx 2590$

Apply 4

1 Get Real!

In the example above, find to the nearest 10 the number of bacteria after:

   a 4 hours

   b two and a half hours

   c 45 minutes

   d one day.

2 Get Real!

David puts £500 into a savings account that pays 4% per year in interest, added once a year.
The interest is added onto the money in the account.
How much will David have in the account at the end of:

   a 1 year

   b 2 years

   c 5 years?

   d How much interest has David gained at the end of 5 years?

Round your answers sensibly.

3 **Get Real!**

A type of bacteria doubles its numbers every hour.
There are 1 million bacteria at the start.

a Find the number of bacteria after:

   i   3 hours

   ii 5 hours

   iii half an hour.

b Use trial and improvement to estimate, in hours and minutes,
the time taken for the number of bacteria to reach 10 million.

4 **Get Real!**

Gavin is offered a job with a starting salary of £18 000 a year with an
annual increase of 2.5%.

a How much will Gavin earn per month after 1 year?

b Will he be earning over £20 000 a year after 5 years?

5 **Get Real!**

Sue puts £500 into a savings account. After a year, she has £515.

a What annual rate of interest is paid on her account?

b How much money will Sue have after 2 years?

c How many years will it take for Sue's money to exceed £550?

6 **Get Real!**

In one part of the country, house prices rose by an average rate of
10% a year for the years 2000–2005.

a What did a house that cost £50 000 in 2000 cost in 2005?

b How much did the price of a house costing £78 000 go up in these
5 years?

c What is the price in 2005 of a house that cost £x in 2000?

7 **Get Real!**

Some banks and building societies add interest on to savings accounts
every 6 months instead of every year. So if the annual rate of interest is
4%, 2% interest is added every 6 months.
Alex puts £800 into an account paying 2% every 6 months.

a How much will Alex have in his account at the end of 1 year?

b How much more is this than if 4% interest had been added at the
end of the year?

c Compare the difference in the interest after 2 years.

d Explain why, with simple interest the total amount of interest is the
same with both methods but with compound interest the amounts of
interest are different.

8 Get Real!

The value of a car depreciates by 10% each year from when it is 4 years old to when it is 8 years old. Its value when it is 4 years old is £3500.

What is its value when it is 8 years old?
Give your answer to a sensible degree of accuracy.

9 Get Real!

Research shows that the number of tigers in India has recently been declining at a rate of approximately 1% per year.
The number of tigers in 2002 was estimated as 3836.

a Calculate the number of tigers in India in 2005 at this rate of decrease.

b How many tigers would be lost in the 10 years from 2002 to 2012?

c Explain why working out 10% of the 3836 does not give the correct answer to part **b**.

10 Get Real!

The area of rainforest in Brazil is declining at an estimated rate of 2.3% each year. The current area of rainforest is 1.8 million square kilometres. According to this estimated rate:

a how many square kilometres will be lost next year

b what will the area of rainforest in Brazil be in 5 years' time?

11 The value of a car depreciated from £8000 to £5000 in 2 years.

a Find the percentage depreciation per year.

b What would a car costing £2250 at the end of the 2 years have been worth at the beginning if it had this percentage rate of depreciation?

12 The price of a house went up from £49 000 to £70 000 in 5 years.

a What is the average annual percentage rate of increase?

b Explain why it is not correct to find the total increase as a percentage of the £49 000 divided by 5.

Explore

If someone puts £100 into a bank that pays 100% interest once a year (very unlikely!) the total amount in the bank at the end of year would be £200

◎ Show that, if the interest was added every 6 months instead of every year, the amount at the end of a year would be £225

◎ What would the amount be at the end of a year if the interest was added every month?

◎ Every week?
Every day?

> **Investigate further**

Learn 5 Direct and inverse proportion

Examples:

The area of a rectangle is fixed. The product of the length and the width is fixed
When the length of the rectangle This means that the length of the rectangle is
is 15 cm, its width is 7.2 cm. inversely proportional to its width

a Find an equation expressing the length of the rectangle in terms of its width.

b Use your equation to find the length of the rectangle when the width is 6 cm.

c Sketch a graph of length against width.

Let the area be A cm², the length l cm and the width w cm.

a
$$A = lw$$
The area is fixed, so the product of
the length and the width is always
the same (constant)

$$l = \frac{A}{w}$$
This equation shows that l is equal

The equation has been rearranged
It is like rearranging the
'distance = speed × time' formula to give
$$speed = \frac{distance}{time}$$

to a constant (A) times $\frac{1}{w}$

In other words, l is **directly**

proportional to $\frac{1}{w}$, or **inversely**

proportional to w
Another way of expressing this is

Since $l = 15$ when $w = 7.2$,

to write $l \propto \frac{1}{w}$

$$15 = \frac{A}{7.2}$$

$\propto$ means 'is proportional to'

Multiplying by 7.2 gives

You could work the area out at the
beginning but this shows the process
of working with inverse proportion

$$A = 15 \times 7.2 = 108$$

So an equation for l in terms of w is

$$l = \frac{108}{w}$$

b When the width is 6 cm, $w = 6$, therefore,

$$l = \frac{108}{6} = 18$$

So, when the width is 6 cm, the length is 18 cm.

c A sketch of length against width is:

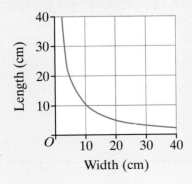

All inverse proportion graphs are
this shape. Notice its symmetry and
that it never actually meets the
x- and y-axes, just gets close to them

Apply 5

1 Get Real!

The amount Emma is paid is directly proportional to the hours she works.
When she works for 6 hours she is paid £33.
Emma is paid £P after working h hours.

  a Find a formula expressing P in terms of h and use it to find:

    i how much Emma will be paid for 8 hours work

    ii how long Emma must work to be paid £110.

  b Sketch a graph of P against h.

  c What does the gradient of the line represent?

2 P is directly proportional to the square root of Q.
If $P = 6$ when $Q = 100$, find a formula expressing P in terms of Q and
use it to find:

  a P when $Q = 64$

  b Q when $P = 3.6$

  c a formula expressing Q in terms of P.

3 The circumference of a circle is directly proportional to its diameter.
A circle with a diameter of 20 cm has a circumference of approximately
62.8 cm.

  a Find a formula connecting C and d, where C cm is the circumference
and d cm is the diameter.

  b Use your formula to find the circumference of a circle with diameter 12 cm.

  c Use your formula to find the diameter of a circle with circumference 1 metre.

4 Get Real!

A petrol pump takes 20 seconds to fill an 8-litre can.
How long will it take to fill a 70-litre car fuel tank?

5 Get Real!

£10 is worth €16.20. Write a formula to find the number of pounds, P,
you get for E euro.

6 If the weight, w grams, of a sphere is directly proportional to the radius,
r cm, cubed, then when the radius is 2 cm the weight is 4 grams.
Find the weight of a sphere with a radius of 5 cm.

7 Get Real!

The amount that Sajid earns, £P, is directly proportional to the number
of hours, n, for which he works.
When he worked for 8 hours he was paid £30.

  a Find an equation connecting P and n.

  b How much will he be paid for 10 hours work at the same rate of pay?

  c Sketch a graph of P against n.

  d What are the links between this question and Apply **3** question **2**?

8 Get Real!

The number of days a food supply lasts is inversely proportional to the number of people to be fed. You have enough food for 5 people for 7 days.
How long will the food last if there are only 2 people?

 9 In each part of this question, the two variables x and y are inversely proportional.
Use the given pair of values of x and y to find the constant k in the equation. Then use the equation to find the missing x- or y-value. Round off sensibly when necessary.

   a When $x = 5$, $y = 12$. Find y when x is 10

   b When $x = 2.5$, $y = 24$. Find x when y is 10

   c When $x = 0.1$, $y = 10$. Find y when x is 0.2

   d When $x = \frac{1}{10}$, $y = 10$. Find x when y is $\frac{1}{5}$

   e When $x = 0.53$, $y = 2.6$. Find y when x is 0.72

10 Two quantities are inversely proportional.
If one quantity is doubled, what happens to the other?
Illustrate your answer with an example.

11 Say whether each pair of variables is directly proportional, inversely proportional, or neither.

   a Length and width of a rectangle with fixed perimeter.

   b Length and width of a rectangle with fixed area.

   c Time taken and distance travelled at constant speed.

   d Speed and time taken for a journey of fixed distance.

   e Length and perimeter of square.

   f Length and area of square.

12 Given that $y \propto x$, copy and complete this table.

x	5		40
y	45	180	

13 Match the following:

y is inversely proportional to x	$y = kx^{-3}$
y is proportional to x^3	$y = kx^3$
y is inversely proportional to the square root of x	$\dfrac{k}{\sqrt{x}}$
y is proportional to the cube root of x	$y = \dfrac{k}{x}$
y is inversely proportional to x cubed	$y = x^{\frac{1}{3}}$

14 The diagram below shows these relationships:

  i y is proportional to x

  ii y is proportional to x^2

  iii y is proportional to x^3

  iv y is inversely proportional to x

  v y is proportional to the square root of x

Which relationship matches which graph?

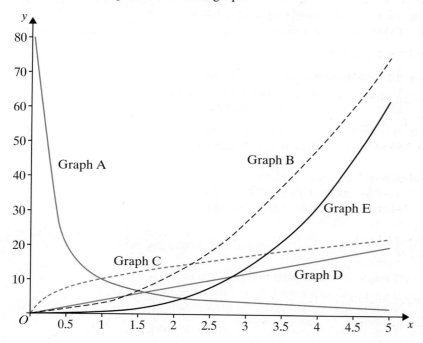

Ratio and proportion

The following exercise tests your understanding of this chapter, with the questions appearing in order of increasing difficulty.

 1 a In a choir there are 12 boys and 18 girls.
Express this as a ratio in its simplest form.

b Two more boys and two more girls join the choir.
Express the new ratio in its simplest form.

2 a 2400 people voted in a local election.
Votes for the three candidates were in the ratio 5 : 6 : 9.
How many votes did each candidate get?

b A drink is made up of water, orange and lemon in the ratio 5 : 1 : 2.
Find the amount of water, orange and lemon in a 1 litre bottle.

3 a Jamie is cooking omelettes.
To make omelettes for 4 people he uses 6 eggs.
How many eggs does Jamie need to make omelettes
for 10 people?

b The supermarkets 'Lessprice' and 'Lowerpay' both sell
packs of pens.
'Lessprice' sells a pack of 5 pens for £1.25
'Lowerpay' sells a pack of 6 of the same pens for £1.44
Which supermarket gives the greater value?

c Two circles have radii of 5 cm and 6 cm respectively.
What is the ratio of:

i their circumferences

ii their areas?

d It takes Kelly 25 seconds to run 200 m.
At the same pace, how long will it take her to run:

i 56 m

ii 128 m?

4 a Due to illness, a man increases his weight each year in the ratio $10:11$.
When diagnosed he weighed 13 stones.
How heavy was he at the end of the third year?

b Mr Clumsy has dropped oil onto his carpet.
The area of the stain is increasing in the ratio of $5:6$ each minute.
The original stain was 50 cm^2.
How big is the stain after 3 minutes?

c A car, originally bought for £10 000, depreciates at a rate of 30% yearly.
How much is it worth after 4 years?

5 a If $a = kb^2$ you say that a is proportional to b^2.
Express the following equations in a similar way:

i $A = \pi r^2$

ii $v = \frac{4}{3}\pi r^3$

iii $y = \dfrac{5}{x^2}$

iv $T = \frac{3}{4}\sqrt{l}$

b Christopher Columbus is h m above sea level.
The distance, d km, that he can see to the horizon is proportional
to the square root of the height.
When Christopher is 100 m above sea level the horizon is 36 km away.
Calculate:

i the distance to the horizon when Christopher is 150 m
above sea level

ii how far up Christopher must go to be able to see 40 km
out to sea

iii how much further Christopher can see when he climbs
from a height of 81 m to 121 m above sea level.

c Boyle's law states that, under certain conditions, the pressure
exerted by a particular mass of gas is inversely proportional to
the volume it occupies.
In these conditions a volume of 150 cm^3 exerts a pressure of
$6 \times 10^4 \text{ Nm}^{-2}$.
The volume is reduced to 80 cm^3.
What is the new pressure?

6 These five sketch graphs show proportional relationships.

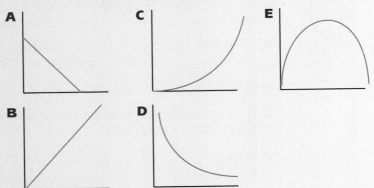

Match each of these statements with an appropriate graph.

   i The distance a stone falls down a well is proportional to the square of the time it takes.

   ii The price of a piece of wood is proportional to its length.

  iii The time taken to drive a set distance is inversely proportional to the average speed.

9 Use of symbols

OBJECTIVES

D ➤ **Examiners would normally expect students who get a D grade to be able to:**

Multiply out expressions with brackets such as $3(x + 2)$ or $5(x - 2)$

Factorise expressions such as $6a + 8$ and $x^2 - 3x$

C ➤ **Examiners would normally expect students who get a C grade also to be able to:**

Expand (and simplify) harder expressions such as $x(x^2 - 5)$ and $3(x + 2) - 5(2x - 1)$

B ➤ **Examiners would normally expect students who get a B grade also to be able to:**

Expand (and simplify) quadratic expressions such as $(x + 4)(x - 2)$, $(2x + y)(3x - 2y)$ and $(x + 2)^2$

Factorise quadratic expressions such as $4x^2 + 6xy$ and $x^2 - 8x - 16$

Simplify rational expressions such as $\dfrac{2(x + 1)^2}{x + 1}$

A ➤ **Examiners would normally expect students who get an A grade also to be able to:**

Factorise harder quadratic expressions such as $a^2 - 16b^2$ and $5x^2 + 13x - 6$

A* ➤ **Examiners would normally expect students who get an A* grade also to be able to:**

Factorise harder quadratic expressions such as $x^2 - 10x + a$, writing them in the form $(x + b)^2 + c$

Simplify harder rational expressions such as $\dfrac{x^2 + 2x}{x^2 - 4}$

What you should already know ...

■ Add, subtract and multiply integers

■ Multiply a two-digit number by a single-digit number

■ Simplify expressions with more than one variable such as $2a + 5b + a - 2b$

Variable – a symbol representing a quantity that can take different values such as x, y or z

Term – a number, variable or the product of a number and a variable(s) such as 3, x or $3x$

Algebraic expression – a collection of terms separated by + and − signs such as $x + 2y$ or $a^2 + 2ab + b^2$

Product – the result of multiplying together two (or more) numbers, variables, terms or expressions

Collect like terms – to group together terms of the same variable, for example, $2x + 4x + 3y = 6x + 3y$

Consecutive – in sequence

Simplify – to make simpler by collecting like terms

Expand – to remove brackets to create an equivalent expression (expanding is the opposite of factorising)

Factorise – to include brackets by taking common factors (factorising is the opposite of expanding)

Linear expression – a combination of terms where the highest power of the variable is 1

Linear expressions	Non-linear expressions
x	x^2
$x + 2$	$\frac{1}{x}$
$3x + 2$	$3x^2 + 2$
$3x + 4y$	$(x + 1)(x + 2)$
$2a + 3b + 4c + \ldots$	x^3

Quadratic expression – an expression containing terms where the highest power of the variable is 2

Quadratic expressions	Non-quadratic expressions
x^2	x
$x^2 + 2$	$2x$
$3x^2 + 2$	$\frac{1}{x}$
$4 + 4y^2$	$3x^2 + 5x^3$
$(x + 1)(x + 2)$	$x(x + 1)(x + 2)$

Rational expression – a fraction, for example,

$$\frac{x^2 - 9}{x + 3}$$

Coefficient – the number (with its sign) in front of the letter representing the unknown, for example:

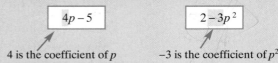

4 is the coefficient of p −3 is the coefficient of p^2

Equation – a statement showing that two expressions are equal, for example, $2y - 7 = 15$

Formula – an equation showing the relationship between two or more variables, for example, $E = mc^2$

Identity – two expressions linked by the $\equiv$ sign are true for all values of the variable, for example, $3x + 3 \equiv 3(x + 1)$

Learn 1   Expanding brackets

Examples:

a Expand $5(2y - 1)$.

	$2y$	-1
5	$10y$	-5

$5 \times -1 = -5$

$5(2y - 1) = \boxed{10y - 5}$ Write $10y - 5$ not $10y + -5$

$10y - 5$ is a linear expression because the highest power of the variable (y) is 1.

b Expand $2p(p^2 - 5)$.

	p^2	-5
2p	$2p^3$	$-10p$

$2p \times -5 = -10p$

$2p(p^2 - 5) = 2p^3 - 10p$

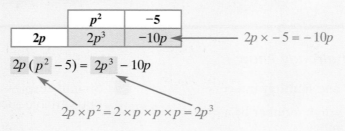

$2p \times p^2 = 2 \times p \times p \times p = 2p^3$

c Expand and simplify $3(x - 2) - 5(2x - 1)$.

> Treat this as two separate algebraic expressions, $3(x - 2)$ and $-5(2x - 1)$ and merge the answers together at the end

Step 1 Expand $3(x - 2)$.

	x	-2
3	$3x$	-6

$3(x - 2) = 3x - 6$

Step 2 Expand $-5(2x - 1)$.

	$2x$	-1
-5	$-10x$	$+5$

$\leftarrow \quad -5 \times -1 = +5$

$-5(2x - 1) = -10x + 5$

Step 3 Merge the two answers by collecting like terms:

$3(x - 2) - 5(2x - 1) = \underline{3x} \,\boxed{-6} - \underline{10x} \,\boxed{+5}$
$= -7x - 1$

> Underlining or circling like terms (including their sign) helps when collecting them:
> $3x - 10x = -7x$ and $-6 + 5 = -1$

Apply 1

1 Multiply these out:

a $4(x + 2)$

b $6(y + 3)$

c $3(3 + 2y)$

d $7(g - 4)$

e $5(2d - 3)$

f $8(5f - 1)$

g $\frac{1}{2}(4b + 6)$

h $\frac{1}{4}(16f - 4)$

i $\dfrac{35h + 10}{5}$

j $\frac{3}{4}(12a - 28)$

k $-4(q + 2)$

l $-5(2m - 3)$

m $-7(-4a - 1)$

2 Sam thinks the answer to $5(3x - 2)$ is $15x - 2$. Hannah says he is wrong. Who is correct and why?

3 Expand:

a $p(p + 3)$

b $b(b - 4)$

c $2a(a + 5)$

d $x(x^3 + 3)$

e $4d(1 - 2d)$

f $\dfrac{m}{3}(m - 9)$

g $\dfrac{2h}{3}(3h + 6)$

h $w(ig + am)$

i $t(t^2 - 1)$

j $x^2(4 + x^3)$

k $y^2(y^5 + 4y^3)$

l $2y^2(4y - 2y^3)$

m $4p^2q(3pq + 2q)$

n $2ab\left(\dfrac{4}{a} + \dfrac{1}{2b}\right)$

4 The answer is $12y - 36$.
Write down five questions of the form $a(by + c)$ with this answer.
(a, b, and c are integers – positive or negative numbers.)

5 Expand and simplify:

a $4(x + 2) + 2(x + 3)$

d $3(m - 1) - 4(m - 2)$

g $4(t - 2) - 2(t + 1)$

b $2(p + 3) + 3(2p - 4)$

e $\frac{1}{2}(6y - 3) + \frac{1}{4}(12 - 4y)$

c $6x - (2 - x)$

f $4x - (x + 2)$

6 Simplify:

a $4(2m - 3) + 3(m - 6)$

d $4(2y - 1) - 4(3y - 5)$

g $2x(2x + 3) - 5x(3x + 4)$

b $3(2a - 1) - 3(4 - a)$

e $5(2t - 4) - 7(2 - 3t)$

c $5(6x - 3) + 2(3 - 2x)$

f $\frac{x}{2}(3x - 4) + \frac{x}{4}(2x - 8)$

7 Josie thinks the answer to $3(2m - 1) - 4(m - 2)$ is $2m - 11$.
Explain what she has done wrong.

8 Find the integers a and b if $4(x - a) - b(x - 1) = 2x - 14$.

9

A $3y + 2$	**B** $2y - 3$	**C** $5y - 1$	**D** $y + 2$

Expand and simplify:

a $2\mathbf{A} + 3\mathbf{C}$ **b** $\mathbf{C} - 2\mathbf{D}$ **c** $2\mathbf{A} - \mathbf{B}$

d Work out a combination of two cards that gives the answer 13.

10 Get Real!
The diagram shows an L-shaped floor with dimensions as shown.
The floor is to be covered with tiles, each measuring 1 m by 1 m.

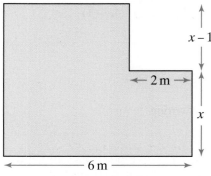

a By splitting the floor into two rectangles, calculate the area of the floor.

b By splitting the floor into two different rectangles, calculate the area of the floor.

Are your answers the same each time?
Give a reason for your answer.

11 The answer is $2y + 3$.
Find five questions of the form $a(by + c) \pm d(ey + f)$ with this answer.
(a, b, c, d, e and f are all integers.)

Explore

◎ Think of a number
◎ Add 2
◎ Multiply the new total by 4
◎ Halve your answer
◎ Subtract twice the original number
◎ The answer is 4

(Investigate further)

Explore

◎ Pick a blue card
◎ Double the number
◎ Add 1 to the new number
◎ Multiply the new number by 5
◎ Pick a white card
◎ Add this number to the previous result
◎ Subtract 5
◎ What do you notice?

5	6	7	8
1	2	3	4

(Investigate further)

Learn 2   Expanding linear expressions

Examples:

a Expand and simplify $(x + 4)(x - 2)$.

	x	$+4$
x	x^2	$+4x$
-2	$-2x$	-8

Remember:
$-2 \times 4 = -8$

$(x + 4)(x - 2) = x^2 \boxed{+ 4x - 2x} - 8$
$= x^2 + 2x - 8$

Underlining or circling like terms
($+4x$ and $-2x$ in this example) helps
when simplifying your answer

b Expand and simplify $(2x + y)(3x - 2y)$.

$2x \times -2y = -4xy$ because
$2 \times -2 = -4$ and $x \times y = xy$

	$2x$	$+y$
$3x$	$6x^2$	$+3xy$
$-2y$	$-4xy$	$-2y^2$

$(2x + y)(3x - 2y) = 6x^2 + 3xy - 4xy - 2y^2$
$= 6x^2 - xy - 2y^2$

Write $3xy - 4xy$ as $-xy$
rather than $-1xy$

89

Apply 2

1 Expand and simplify:

a $(x+3)(x+2)$

b $(y+3)(y+4)$

c $(b+5)(b+1)$

d $(a+4)(a-5)$

e $(m+2)(m-6)$

f $(h-4)(h+8)$

g $(3-x)(x+7)$

h $(x-3)(x+3)$

i $(2x+4)(x+2)$

j $(p-4)(p-3)$

k $(2y+3)(3y-4)$

l $(2-t)(t-3)$

m $(4-a)(5-a)$

n $(x+2)^2$

o $(y-3)^2$

p $(d+5)(d-5)$

q $(d-1)(d-2)$

r $(2p+4)^2$

s $(5k-2)^2$

2 Katya thinks the answer to $(x-2)(x+3)$ is x^2+x+1.
Becky thinks the answer is x^2+x-6.
Who is correct and why?

3 Paul thinks the answer to $(x+3)^2$ is x^2+9. Is he correct?
Give a reason for your answer.

4 a The answer is x^2+8x+c where c is an integer.

Find five questions in the form $(x+a)(x+b)$ where a and b are integers.

b The answer is $x^2+dx+48$ where d is an integer.

Find five questions in the form $(x+e)(x+f)$ where e and f are integers.

c The answer is $60+gx-x^2$ where g is an integer.

Find five questions in the form $(h-x)(k+x)$ where h and k are integers.

5 Calculate 102^2-98^2 without a calculator.

6 Find the integers p and q if $(x-p)(x+q)=x^2-3x-10$.

HINT Use the answer from question **1**, part **h** to help you.

7

| **A** $y+2$ | **B** $y-3$ | **C** $y-1$ | **D** $y+3$ |

Expand and simplify:

a AC   **b** CD   **c** DC   **d** B²

e Work out a product of two cards that gives the answer y^2-9.

8 Show that $(n-2)^2+2(n-2)+2n=n^2$.

9 Get Real!

Farmer Forgetful can't remember the exact dimensions of his field. He has found a scrap of paper with the following sketch:

$x + 15$

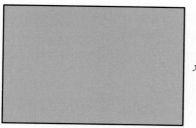

$x + 10$

a Write an expression for the area of the field.

Farmer Forgetful has forgotten he needs two separate fields, so he divides his field like this:

$x + 15$

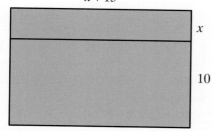

x

10

b Write an expression for the area of each new field.

c Write an expression for the total area of the two fields.

d By expanding and simplifying the expressions for parts **a** and **c**, show that the total area of land is the same in each case.

10 The answer is $3x^2 + gx + 12$ where g is an integer.
Find five questions in the form $(mx + n)(x + p)$ where m, n and p are integers.
State the value of g in each case.

11 Expand and simplify:

a $(3x + 2y)(x + y)$ **e** $(3x - y)(x - y)$ **i** $(c + d)^2$

b $(2p + q)(3p + 2q)$ **f** $(b - 3c)(b + 3c)$ **j** $(3x + y)^2$

c $(2a - b)(4a + b)$ **g** $(2x - 4)(2x + 4)$ **k** $(5p - q)^2$

d $(3p + 2q)(2p - 2q)$ **h** $(6t - 2s)(3t - 4s)$ **l** $(4w - 3v)^2$

12 The answer is $6x^2 + fx + 12$ where f is an integer.
Find five questions in the form $(mx + n)(px + q)$ where m, n, p and q are integers.
State the value of f in each case.

Explore

◎ Pick three consecutive even numbers

◎ Multiply them together

◎ Is the total a multiple of 8?

> **HINT** How do you write an expression in n that is always even? What would the next even number be?

Investigate further

Explore

◎ Pick two cards from the list below:

| 1 | 2 | 3 | 4 | 5 | 6 | 7 | 8 | 9 | 10 |

◎ The cards are designed so that the number on the back is the complement in 20, that is, on the back of 2 the number is 18

◎ Multiply the top number of card 1 by the reverse number of card 2

◎ Multiply the reverse number of card 1 by the reverse number of card 2

◎ Multiply the top number of card 2 by 20

◎ Add the three totals

◎ Try again with two other cards

> **HINT** If the top number of a card is x, what can you say about the reverse number?

Investigate further

Learn 3　Factorising expressions

Examples:

a Factorise $5a - 10$

$5a - 10 = 5\ (a - 2)$

$5a = \boxed{5} \times a$ and $10 = 2 \times \boxed{5}$
Both terms have 5 as a common factor

b Factorise $12s^2t - 16s$

$12s^2t - 16s = 4s\ (3st - 4)$

$12s^2t = 3 \times \boxed{4 \times s} \times s \times t$ and $16s = 8 \times 2 \times s$
Or $12s^2t = 6 \times 2 \times s \times s \times t$ and $16s = 4 \times \boxed{4 \times s}$
Both terms have s as a common factor and 4 as the highest common factor

> **HINT** You can always check if you have factorised correctly by multiplying the bracket out to make sure you get the question.

Treat factorising as the 'reverse' of expanding.

Apply 3

1 Factorise the following expressions:

HINT Two of these expressions cannot be factorised.

a $2x + 6$

b $3y + 12$

c $7y - 63$

d $8y - 40$

e $14y + 20$

f $6t - 18$

g $21 - 42t$

h $44t - 55c$

i $13a + 23b$

j $20b + 35a + 15c$

k $-12a - 16$

l $-42ab + 70cd + 14ef$

m $18f - 36g + 12h$

n $20xy + 60tu - 80pq$

o $2f - 11g + 33h$

2 Sandra thinks that $12a + 18$ factorised completely is $3(4a + 6)$.
Is she correct? Explain your answer.

3 The answer is $4(... p + ...)$ where $... p + ...$ is an expression.
Find five expressions that can be factorised completely with answers in this form.

4 Rashid thinks he has factorised $2x + 3y$ correctly as $2(x + 1\frac{1}{2}y)$.
Rana thinks the expression cannot be factorised.
Who is correct and why?

5 Factorise the following expressions:

a $2ab + 5b$

b $3xy + 5xz$

c $p^2 + 2p$

d $x^2 - 3x$

e $4x^2 + 6xy$

f $a^2 - a$

g $6xy + 7xyz$

h $y^3 - 2y^2$

i $wig - wam$

j $bugs + bunny$

k $hocus - pocus$

l $silly + billy$

m $wonkey - donkey$

n $2p^2q^3 + 5pq^2$

o $7m^2n^3 + 11m^3n^2p + 3m^4n^3q$

p $m^2uf^2c^3 + 3mu^3f^4c$

6 Get Real!
Sanjit and Anna are playing snooker. They notice that the red balls fit inside the triangle in the following pattern:
1, 3, 6, 10, 15, ...

Sanjit uses a method of differences and finds the nth term to be $\frac{1}{2}n^2 + \frac{1}{2}n$.

The expression gives the 5th triangular number as 15 (test it!) which is correct.

Factorise Sanjit's expression to find another expression for the nth triangular number.

7 Kenny thinks that when $4x^2y + 6xy^2$ is factorised completely the answer is $xy(4x + 6y)$. Is he correct? Justify your answer.

8 Factorise completely the following expressions:

a $4xy + 6x$

b $3cd + 12d^2$

c $24gh - 4g$

d $3pq^2r + 12p^2q$

e $28f^2g^2h^2 - 21f^2gh^3$

f $72p^2q + 32pqr^2 - 48q^2rs^2$

g $5x^2yz + 15xy^3z^2$

h $13s^2t^2u^2 + 91s^2t^2u$

i $12ab^2c^3d^4 - 14a^4b^3c^2d$

j $6a^2bc - 9ab^2c^2d$

k $3(a + b)^2 + 4(a + b)$

l $6(x + y)^2 - 4(x + y)$

m $(2p + q)^3 + 5(2p + q)^2$

n $3(2x + y) - 8x - 4y$

9 Copy these two tables.
Match the expression with the correct factorisation buddy.
Fill in the missing buddies.

Expression
$2x^2 + 8x$
$6x^2y - 3xy$

Factorisation
$2x(x + 4)$
$3xy(2y - 1)$
$x(x + 8)$

10 Charles thinks that $xy + 2x + 2y + 4$ cannot be factorised completely.
Chica says it can. Who is correct? Justify your answer.

11 Factorise the following expressions completely:

a $ab - 2a + 3b - 6$ **c** $8fg + 12f + 6g + 9$ **e** $2p^2q + 2p^2t - q^2 - qt$

b $2x - 6 + yx - 3y$ **d** $4ab - 8a - 3b + 6$ **f** $12wy + 9y + 4w + 3$

Explore

◎　Pick four consecutive odd numbers

◎　Add them together

◎　Is the answer a multiple of 8?

◎　Investigate further by picking four other consecutive odd numbers

HINT　How do you write an expression in n that is always odd? What would the next odd number be?

Investigate further

Learn 4　Factorising quadratic expressions

Examples:　**a** Factorise $x^2 + 7x + 12$.

$$x^2 + 7x + 12 = (x + 4)(x + 3)$$

Numbers that give a product of 12:

1×12　　-1×-12
2×6　　-2×-6
(3×4)　　-3×-4

Only these two numbers add up to 7

	x	$+3$
x	x^2	$+3x$
$+4$	$+4x$	12

Sum = $7x$

The numbers in the two green cells have to give a product of 12

The two blue cells have to give a sum of $7x$

b Factorise $2p^2 + 5p + 2$.

$$2p^2 + 5p + 2 = (2p + 1)(p + 2)$$

Check:

- $2p \times p = 2p^2$
- $1 \times 2 = 2$
- $2p \times 2 + p \times 1 = 5p$

$(2p + 1)(p + 2)$

Note: $(2p + 2)(p + 1)$ would give $2p \times 1 + p \times 2 = 4p$ not $5p$

$2p^2 + 5p + 2$ is a quadratic expression because the highest power of the variable, p, is 2.
The coefficient of p^2 is 2, and the coefficient of p is 5.

c Factorise $x^2 - 10x + 3$ and write it in the form $(x + b)^2 + c$.

$$(x + b)^2 + c = x^2 + 2bx + b^2 + c$$

So comparing:

Expanding:

	x	$+b$
x	x^2	$+bx$
$+b$	$+bx$	$+b^2$

$$x^2 + 2bx + b^2 + c = x^2 - 10x + 3$$

$$+ 2bx = -10x \qquad b^2 + c = 3$$
$$2b = -10 \qquad 25 + c = 3$$
$$b = -5 \qquad c = -22 \qquad \text{As } b = -5$$

So $x^2 - 10x + 9 = (x - 5)^2 - 22$

Factorising is the 'reverse' of expanding.

> **HINT** You can always check if you have factorised correctly by multiplying the bracket out to make sure you get back to the question.

Apply 4

1 Factorise completely:

a $x^2 + 5x + 6$

b $x^2 + 8x + 7$

c $x^2 + 8x + 12$

d $y^2 + 14y + 49$

e $b^2 + 8b + 15$

f $p^2 + 22p + 21$

g $x^2 + 17x + 42$

h $d^2 + 13d + 42$

i $x^2 + 11x + 18$

j $w^2 + 2w + 8$

k $x^2 + 8x$

> **HINT** One of these expressions cannot be factorised.

2 Billie thinks that $x^2 + 7x + 8$ can be factorised to $(x + 7)(x + 1)$ because $7 \times x$ gives the $7x$ and $7 + 1$ gives the 8 at the end. Is she correct?

3 Factorise:

a $y^2 + y - 6$

b $t^2 - t - 6$

c $p^2 - 5p - 6$

d $x^2 - 8x - 9$

e $b^2 - 12b - 13$

f $x^2 + 2x - 35$

g $x^2 - 5x - 24$

h $d^2 + 10d - 11$

i $y^2 + 4y - 12$

j $x^2 - 25$

k $p^2 - 100$

l $y^2 - 225$

m $x^2 - a^2$

n $6 - x - x^2$

o $15 + 2x - x^2$

4 Calculate the following, without using a calculator.

a $78^2 - 22^2$

b $59^2 - 41^2$

c $8.25^2 - 1.75^2$

d $0.62^2 - 0.38^2$

> **HINT** Use the answer to **3j** to help you.

5 The answer is $(x + 2)(x - a)$ where a is an integer.
Find five quadratic expressions that can be factorised to give this answer.

6 Are $(x - 6)$ and $(x + 2)$ the factors of $x^2 + 4x - 12$?
If they are not, find the correct factors.

7 Factorise:

a $x^2 - 10x + 25$

b $y^2 - 14y + 13$

c $d^2 - 14d + 48$

d $p^2 - 9p + 20$

e $t^2 - 13t + 36$

f $a^2 - 7a + 12$

g $x^2 - 16x + 28$

h $b^2 - 28b + 27$

i $x^2 - 11x + 30$

j $k^2 - 18k + 56$

k $y^2 - y + 5$

> **HINT** One of these expressions cannot be factorised.

8

| A $x^2 + 6x + 8$ | B $x^2 + 4x + 4$ | C $x^2 + 3x + 2$ | D $x^2 - 4$ |

a What factor do all four quadratic expressions have in common?

b Which quadratic expression is the difference of two squares?

c Which quadratic expression has a repeated factor?

9 Factorise:

a $x^2 + 13x + 40$

b $y^2 - 17y + 60$

c $b^2 - 10b + 21$

d $p^2 + 12p + 11$

e $x^2 + 3x$

f $y^2 - 27y$

g $x^2 - 49$

h $x^2 + 36$

i $y^2 - 3y - 18$

j $b^2 - 8b + 16$

> **HINT** One of these expressions cannot be factorised.

10 Copy the tables.
Match the quadratic expression with the correct factorisation buddy.
Fill in the missing buddies.

Quadratic expression
$x^2 + 13x + 40$
$x^2 - 81$
$x^2 + 16$
$x^2 - 13x + 40$

Factorisation
$(x - 9)^2$
$(x + 4)^2$
$(x + 8)(x + 5)$
Cannot be factorised

11 Copy and fill in the gaps.

a $x^2 - \square x - 12 = (x - 3)(x + \square)$

b $x^2 + 5x - \square = (x - 3)(x + \square)$

c $x^2 + 14x + \square = (x + \square)^2$

d $x^2 - \square x + 16 = (x - \square)^2$

12 Get Real!

Bob and Pam are investigating the number sequence of piles of cannonballs: 1, 4, 10, 20, ...
Using a method of differences, Bob finds the expression for the nth term to be $\frac{1}{6}n^3 + \frac{1}{2}n^2 + \frac{1}{3}n$.
Pam searches the internet and discovers that the numbers are called tetrahedral numbers and the nth term is $\frac{1}{6}n(n+1)(n+2)$.
Bob prefers Pam's expression.
Factorise Bob's expression into Pam's expression.

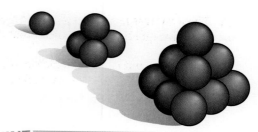

HINT Write all the fractions with the same denominator.

13 $x^2 + bx + a = (x+c)^2$ where a, b and c are integers.
Find five different sets of values for a, b and c to make the statement correct.

14 Christopher notices that the coefficient of x^2 in quadratic expressions is not always one. He reckons he can factorise other quadratic expressions, for example:

a $2x^2 + 7x + 6 = (2x+2)(x+3)$ because $2 \times 3 = 6$

b $3x^2 - x - 2 = (3x+2)(x-1)$ because $2 \times -1 = -2$

c $5x^2 - 14x + 8 = (5x-2)(x-4)$ because $-2 \times -4 = 8$

d $6x^2 + 16x + 8 = (2x+2)(3x+4)$ because $2 \times 4 = 8$

Expand Christopher's expressions and say whether he has factorised the quadratic expressions correctly. If he has not, say which coefficients are incorrect.

15 Factorise completely:

a $2x^2 + 7x + 3$

b $3x^2 + 14x + 8$

c $5x^2 + 8x + 3$

d $2x^2 - x - 1$

e $7x^2 - 27x - 4$

f $5x^2 - 17x + 6$

g $4x^2 - 9$

h $16x^2 - 4$

i $2x^2 - 18$

j $20x^2 - 80$

k $6x^2 - x - 1$

l $8x^2 + 10x + 3$

m $6x^2 - x - 5$

n $10x^2 - 2x - 12$

o $12x^2 - 14x - 6$

p $9x^2 - 18x + 5$

q $6x^2 + 8x - 8$

r $4x^2 - 10x - 6$

s $15x^2 - 39x - 18$

t $6 + x - 2x^2$

u $15 + 4x - 3x^2$

v $12 - 2x - 4x^2$

16 Copy the tables.
Match the quadratic expression with the correct factorisation.
Fill in the missing buddies.

Quadratic expression
$2x^2 + 5x + 3$
$3x^2 - 5x - 2$
$16x^2 - 9$

Factorisation
$(2x+1)(x+3)$
$(4x-3)(4x+3)$
$(3x-2)(x+1)$

Learn 5 Simplifying algebraic fractions

You can simplify fractions by factorising and dividing by common factors.

Examples:

a Simplify $\dfrac{x^2 - 2x}{x - 2}$ ← This is a rational expression (that is, a fraction) It has a numerator and a denominator

$\dfrac{x^2 - 2x}{x - 2} = \dfrac{x(x - 2)}{x - 2}$ ← Factorise the numerator

$= x$ ← After dividing the numerator and denominator by $(x - 2)$

b Simplify $\dfrac{x^2 + 6x + 5}{x + 5}$

$\dfrac{x^2 + 6x + 5}{x + 5} = \dfrac{(x + 5)(x + 1)}{x + 5}$ ← Dividing the numerator and denominator by $(x + 5)$

$= x + 1$

c Simplify $\dfrac{3x^2 + 2x - 1}{x^2 - 1}$

$\dfrac{3x^2 + 2x - 1}{x^2 - 1} = \dfrac{(3x - 1)(x + 1)}{(x - 1)(x + 1)}$ ← Factorise the numerator and the denominator

$= \dfrac{3x - 1}{x - 1}$ ← Dividing the numerator and denominator by $(x + 1)$

Apply 5

1 Simplify these expressions.

a $\dfrac{x^2 + 3x}{x + 3}$

b $\dfrac{x^2 + 7x + 10}{x + 2}$

c $\dfrac{x^2 + 4x + 3}{x + 1}$

d $\dfrac{x^2 + 2x}{x^2 - 4}$

e $\dfrac{x^2 + 6x + 5}{x^2 + 8x + 15}$

f $\dfrac{x^2 - 9}{x + 3}$

g $\dfrac{2(x + 1)^2}{x + 1}$

2 Simplify these expressions.

a $\dfrac{2x^2 + 5x - 3}{x + 3}$

b $\dfrac{3x^2 + 7x - 6}{x + 3}$

c $\dfrac{4x^2 + 2x}{2x^2 - 5x - 3}$

d $\dfrac{5x^2 + 7x - 6}{2(x + 2)^2}$

e $\dfrac{3x^2 - 11x + 6}{2x^2 - 5x - 3}$

f $\dfrac{3x^2 - 10x + 8}{18x^2 - 32}$

g $\dfrac{2x^2 - x - 15}{4x^2 - 25}$

Explore

This is a proof that $1 = -1$

Let	$a = 1$ (∗)
Square both sides:	$a^2 = 1$
Subtract 1 from both sides:	$a^2 - 1 = 0$
Factorise:	$(a + 1)(a - 1) = 0$
Divide by $(a - 1)$:	$a + 1 = 0$
Subtract 1 from both sides:	$a = -1$
	but from (∗) $a = 1$
	so $1 = -1$

Obviously, this cannot be true

Investigate further

Use of symbols

ASSESS

The following exercise tests your understanding of this chapter, with the questions appearing in order of increasing difficulty.

1 Remove the brackets from the following expressions.

   a $2(a + 3)$ **e** $7(a + 2b)$ **i** $-6(4a - 3b)$

   b $5(3a - 1)$ **f** $5(6a - 3b)$ **j** $-2(a - 2b + 3)$

   c $-3(4a + 5)$ **g** $-3(3a + 2b)$

   d $-7(3a - 6)$ **h** $-7(3a - 2b)$

2 Factorise the following expressions.

   a $2a + 10$ **f** $10j + 15k - 20l$ **k** $4a^2 - 6a$

   b $10b - 12$ **g** $30p - 45q - 75r$ **l** $bil + ben$

   c $16 - 4c$ **h** $5x + 15y$ **m** $abra + cadabra$

   d $5d + 20e + 35f$ **i** $2ab - 3a$ **n** $12cat + 3sat - 6mat$

   e $6g - 9h + 12i$ **j** $x^2 + 7x$

3 Remove the brackets from the following expressions and simplify.

   a $2c + 3(c + 5)$ **h** $5(2c - 3) - 3(2c - 1)$

   b $2c - 3(c + 5)$ **i** $3(2c - d + 3e) + (5c + 3d - 2e)$

   c $2c + 3(c - 5)$ **j** $3(2c - d + 3e) - (5c + 3d - 2e)$

   d $2c - 3(c - 5)$ **k** $y(y^2 - 7)$

   e $4(c - 3) + 2(c + 7)$ **l** $2z(5z^2 + 4z - 8)$

   f $4(c - 3) - 2(c + 7)$ **m** $x(x - 3) + 5(x - 3)$

   g $5(2c - 3) - 3(2c + 1)$ **n** $p(p^2 + 3p - 4) - 6(p^2 + 3p - 4)$

4 Remove the brackets from the following expressions and simplify.

a $(a+3)(a+9)$ **d** $(y-7)(y-9)$ **g** $(5y-2)(2y-3)$

b $(b+7)(b-2)$ **e** $(x+5)^2$ **h** $(s-6)(s+6)$

c $(c+2)(c-5)$ **f** $(2z+8)(3z-4)$ **i** $(4p+3q)(2p-6q)$

5 Factorise the following quadratic expressions.

a a^2+5a+4 **d** $g^2-2g-35$

b c^2-5c+6 **e** w^2-25

c $e^2+6e-16$ **f** $9s^2-49t^2$

g i Write down the areas of the following rectangles: ACEG; ACDH; BCEF; BCDI.

ii Hence write down the area of rectangle HIFG.

iii Explain this result using the diagram.

HINT Look again at question **4h**.

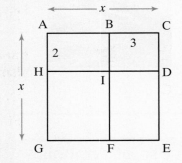

6 Factorise the following quadratic expressions.

a $3x^2+16x+5$ **c** $5x^2-22x+21$ **e** $12+x-6x^2$

b $2x^2-3x-9$ **d** $9g^2-12g+4$

7 David has bought Annwyn a birthday present. It is wrapped in the box shown, which has a square base of length a cm and which is 12 cm tall.

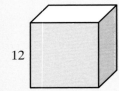

a Write down, in terms of a if necessary:
  i the base area   **ii** the area of a side.

b The total area of the base, four sides and top is 1760 cm^2. Form a quadratic equation and factorise it to find the length of the box.

8 a Copy and complete the following fractions.

i $\dfrac{4a}{5}=\dfrac{}{15}$ **iii** $\dfrac{2c}{3d}=\dfrac{}{12d}$ **v** $\dfrac{e}{f}=\dfrac{ef}{}$

ii $\dfrac{6}{p}=\dfrac{}{5pq}$ **iv** $\dfrac{5}{r}=\dfrac{15s}{}$

b Simplify the following expressions.

i $\dfrac{3ab}{9b}$ **v** $\dfrac{14m^6n^2}{35m^8n}$ **ix** $\dfrac{p^2+2p-15}{p^2-10p+21}$

ii $\dfrac{4a}{6ab}$ **vi** $\dfrac{z^2-z}{(z-1)^2}$ **x** $\dfrac{x^2+x-2}{x^2-x-6}\times\dfrac{x^2+4x-21}{x^2+6x-7}$

iii $\dfrac{12pqr}{9qrs}$ **vii** $\dfrac{4(w+3)}{w^2-9}$

iv $\dfrac{4x^5y}{2x^2y}$ **viii** $\dfrac{x^2-x-12}{x-4}$

10 Quadratic graphs

OBJECTIVES

D **Examiners would normally expect students who get a D grade to be able to:**

Draw graphs of simple quadratic functions such as $y = 3x^2$ and $y = x^2 + 4$

C **Examiners would normally expect students who get a C grade also to be able to:**

Draw graphs of harder quadratic functions such as $y = x^2 - 2x + 1$

Find the points of intersection of quadratic graphs with lines

Use graphs to find the approximate solutions of quadratic equations

A **Examiners would normally expect students who get an A grade also to be able to:**

Use the points of intersection of a quadratic graph such as $y = x^2 - 2x - 4$ with lines such as $y = 2x + 1$ to solve equations like $x^2 - 2x - 4 = 2x + 1$ and simplify this to $x^2 - 4x - 5 = 0$

What you should already know ...

- Add and subtract fractions
- Substitute positive and negative values of x into expressions including squared terms
- Plot graphs from coordinates

VOCABULARY

Variable – a symbol representing a quantity that can take different values such as x, y or z

Quadratic expression – an expression containing terms where the highest power of the variable is 2

Quadratic expressions	Non-quadratic expressions
x^2	x
$x^2 + 2$	$2x$
$3x^2 + 2$	$\frac{1}{x}$
$4 + 4y^2$	$3x^2 + 5x^3$
$(x + 1)(x + 2)$	$x(x + 1)(x + 2)$

Quadratic function – functions like $y = 3x^2, y = 9 - x^2$ and $y = 5x^2 + 2x - 4$ are quadratic functions; they include an x^2 term and may also include x terms and constants

The graphs of quadratic functions are always $\cup$-shaped or $\cap$-shaped

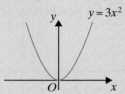

$y = ax^2 + bx + c$ is $\cup$-shaped when a is positive and $\cap$-shaped when a is negative

c is the intercept on the y-axis

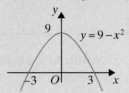

Note that other letters could be used as the variable instead of x (for example, $6t^2 - 3t - 5$ is also a quadratic expression and $h = 30t - 2t^2$ is a quadratic function)

Learn 1   Graphs of simple quadratic functions

Examples:

a Draw the graph of $y = 3x^2$ for values of x from -4 to 4.

b Use the graph to find **i** the value of y when $x = -2.4$
ii the values of x when $y = 35$

a The table below gives the values of y for all integer values of x from -4 to 4.

x	−4	−3	−2	−1	0	1	2	3	4
y	48	27	12	3	0	3	12	27	48

Quadratic functions give curves – you need more points than for linear functions to get the right shape

$3x^2$ means $3 \times x^2$ or $3 \times x \times x$ so when $x = -4$, $3x^2 = 3 \times -4 \times -4 = 48$

The y-values are often symmetrical like this

Check that you can work out the values in the table, with and without your calculator

Plotting these values gives the graph:

Graph of $y = 3x^2$

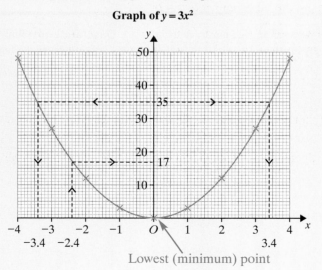

Lowest (minimum) point

The points are joined with a smooth curve

b i From the graph, when $x = -2.4$, $y \approx 17$ ◄———— Remember $\approx$ means 'is approximately equal to'

ii When $y = 35$, there are two possible values of x:
$x = -3.4$ and $x = 3.4$ (to 1 d.p.)

Use your calculator to work out $3x^2$ with each of these values to check how accurate they are

Apply 1

 1 a Draw the graph of $y = x^2$ for values of x from -4 to 4.

b Use your graph to estimate the value of:
i 2.5^2 **ii** $(-1.8)^2$

c Use your graph to estimate the square roots of:
i 13 **ii** 5

 2 a Copy and complete this table for $y = x^2 - 2$

x	-3	-2	-1	0	1	2	3
y	7		-1			2	

b Draw the graph of $y = x^2 - 2$ for values of x from -3 to 3.

c Use your graph to find the value of y when:
i $x = 2.4$ **ii** $x = -1.6$

d Use your graph to find the values of x when:
i $y = 6$ **ii** $y = -0.5$

 3 a Draw the graph of $y = -5x^2$ for values of x from -4 to 4.

b Compare your graph with that of $y = x^2$
What are the similarities and differences?

 4 a Copy and complete the table below for $y = 2x^2 + 3$

x	-4	-3	-2	-1	0	1	2	3	4
$2x^2$	32	18	8		0			18	
$y = 2x^2 + 3$	35		11		3			21	

b Draw the graph of $y = 2x^2 + 3$ for values of x from -4 to 4.

c Give the y-coordinate of the point on the curve with an x-coordinate of:
i 2.5 **ii** -1.5

d Give the x-coordinates of the points on the curve with y-coordinates of:
i 10 **ii** 28

5 The graph shows the function $y = 3x^2 - 5$ for values of x from -4 to 4.

Graph of $y = 3x^2 - 5$

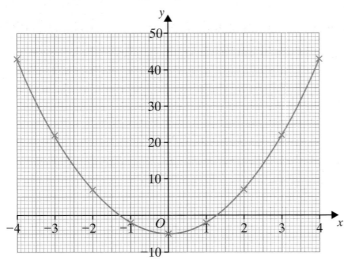

a Use your graph to find the value of y when:
  i $x = 1.8$ **ii** $x = -3.4$

b Use your graph to find the values of x when:
  i $y = 20$ **ii** $y = 36$

c Write the coordinates of the lowest point on the curve.

6 **a** Draw the graph of $y = 10 - x^2$ for values of x from -4 to 4.

  b **i** Give the x-coordinates of the points where the curve crosses the x-axis.

  ii Explain why the answers to part **i** are the square roots of 10.

7 **a** Copy and complete the table below, then use it to draw the graph of $y = (x + 2)(3 - x)$

x	−3	−2	−1	0	0.5	1	2	3	4
x + 2	−1		1		2.5				6
3 − x	6		4		2.5				−1
y = (x + 2)(3 − x)	−6		4		6.25				−6

  b Write down the coordinates of the points where the curve crosses the x-axis.

8 **a** Draw the graph of $y = x(x - 4)$ for values of x from -1 to 5.

  b Write the coordinates of the points where the curve crosses the line $y = 0$

9 Get Real!

The area of the glass in a circular window is given by $A = \pi r^2$, where r is the radius in metres and A is the area in square metres.

a Copy and complete this table, giving values of A to 2 decimal places.

r (m)	0	0.1	0.2	0.3	0.4	0.5	0.6	0.7	0.8	0.9	1.0
$A = \pi r^2$ (m²)			0.13			0.79			2.01		3.14

b Draw a graph of A against r using 2 cm to represent 0.2 on the r-axis and 0.5 on the A-axis.

c Use your graph to estimate the area of the window when the radius is:
  i 0.28 m   **ii** 0.75 m

d Use your graph to estimate the radius of the window when the area is:
  i 2.8 m²   **ii** 1.45 m²

10 The graph shows the points that Paul has plotted for his graph of $y = x^2$

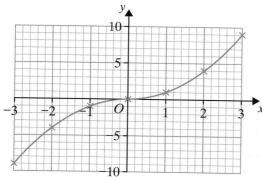

Graph of $y = x^2$

a Is this the shape you would expect?
Give a reason for your answer.

b Complete the table of values for Paul's graph.

x	−3	−2	−1	0	1	2	3
y							

c What mistake has Paul made in calculating the values?

11 The graphs of four quadratic functions are shown in the sketch.

The functions are

  $y = 6x^2$ $y = -6x^2$ $y = x^2 + 6$ $y = x^2 - 6$

Choose the function that represents each curve.

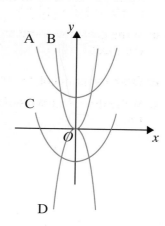

12 a On separate axes draw the graphs of:

  i $y = (x + 1)(x + 3)$

  ii $y = (x - 1)(x - 3)$

  iii $y = (x + 1)(x - 3)$

  iv $y = (x - 1)(x + 3)$

  b What do you notice about your graphs?

13 a Give four possible equations for graph A.

  b Give four possible equations for graph B.

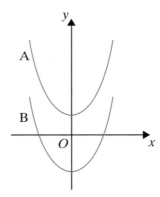

Explore

◎ On the same axes draw the graphs of some functions of the form $y = ax^2$ using both positive and negative values of a (for example, $y = x^2$, $y = 3x^2$ and $y = -3x^2$)
Find out how the graph varies as a varies

◎ On the same axes draw the graphs of some functions of the form $y = x^2 + c$ using both positive and negative values of c (for example, $y = x^2 + 1$, $y = x^2 - 2$); find out how the graph varies as c varies

Investigate further

Learn 2 Graphs of harder quadratic functions

Examples:

  a Draw the graph of $y = 5 + 3x - x^2$ for values of x from -2 to 5.

  b Use the graph to find the solutions of $5 + 3x - x^2 = 0$

  c i Find the x-coordinates of the points where the curve crosses the line $y = 6$
  ii Write a quadratic equation whose solutions are the answers to part **i**.

a The table below gives values for this function.

x	-2	-1	0	1	2	3	4	5
y	-5	1	5	7	7	5	1	-5

The highest value of y in the table is 7, but the curve rises above this between $x = 1$ and 2; to draw the graph accurately it is useful to work out the value of y when $x = 1.5$
When $x = 1.5$, $y = 5 + 3 \times 1.5 - 1.5^2 = 7.25$

b To find the solutions of $5 + 3x - x^2 = 0$ look at the points on $y = 5 + 3x - x^2$ where $y = 0$ (that is, where the curve crosses the x-axis).
The solutions are $x = -1.2$ and $x = 4.2$ (to 1 d.p.)

Graph of $y = 5 + 3x - x^2$

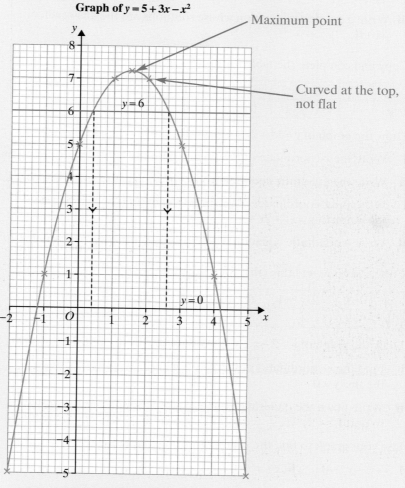

Maximum point

Curved at the top, not flat

c i The graph shows the line $y = 6$
It crosses the curve at the points where $x = 0.4$ and $x = 2.6$ (to 1 d.p.)

ii These are the solutions of the equation $5 + 3x - x^2 = 6$
This equation can also be written as:
$$3x - x^2 = 1 \qquad \text{or} \qquad x^2 - 3x + 1 = 0$$

Apply 2

1 a Copy and complete this table for $y = x^2 - 3x$

x	−1	0	1	2	3	4
y	4			−2		4

b Draw the graph of $y = x^2 - 3x$ for values of x from −1 to 4.

c Use your graph to find the solutions of the equation $x^2 - 3x = 0$

d i Draw the line $y = 3$ on your graph.

ii Find the x-coordinates of the points where the line $y = 3$ crosses the curve $y = x^2 - 3x$

iii Write a quadratic equation whose solutions are the answers to part **ii**.

2 a Copy and complete the table for $y = x^2 + 2x + 1$

x	−4	−3	−2	−1	0	1	2
y	9		1	0		4	

b Draw the graph of $y = x^2 + 2x + 1$ for values of x from −4 to 2.

c i Write the x-coordinate of the point where the curve meets the x-axis.

ii Write the quadratic equation whose solution is the answer to part **i**.

d i Write the x-coordinates of the points where the line $y = 8$ crosses the graph of $y = x^2 + 2x + 1$

ii Write a quadratic equation whose solution is the answer to part **i**.

3 a Copy and complete this table for $y = 5 + x - x^2$

x	−3	−2	−1	0	1	2	3	4
y	−7					3		−7

b Draw the graph of $y = 5 + x - x^2$ for values of x from −3 to 4.

c i Find the x-coordinates of the points where the graph crosses the line $y = 0$

ii Write down the quadratic equation whose solution is the answer to part **i**.

d Use your graph to find the solutions of these equations:

i $3 + x - x^2 = 0$ **ii** $x - x^2 = 0$

4 a Draw the graph of $y = 2x^2 - x - 3$ for $-3 \leqslant x \leqslant +4$

b i Write the x-values where the curve crosses the x-axis.

ii Write the quadratic equation whose solutions are the answers to part **i**.

c i Write the x-values where the curve meets the line $y = 10$

ii Write a quadratic equation whose solutions are the answers to part **i**.

5 Get Real!

A ball is thrown vertically upwards into the air.
After t seconds its height above the ground, h metres, is given by the function $h = 1 + 14t - 5t^2$

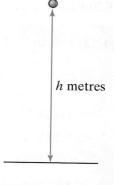

h metres

a Draw the graph of $h = 1 + 14t - 5t^2$ for $0 \leqslant t \leqslant 3$

b Use your graph to find:

   i the height of the ball after 0.25 seconds

   ii how long the ball takes to reach a height of 7.2 metres on its way up

   iii the maximum height reached by the ball and when this occurs

   iv after how long the ball hits the ground.

6 A teacher asks his class to complete a table for $y = 2x^2 - x + 4$

a This is Ella's table but only one of her values for y is correct.

Ella's table

x	-3	-2	-1	0	1	2	3
$2x^2$	36	16	4	0	4	16	36
$-x$	$+3$	$+2$	$+1$	0	-1	-2	-3
$+4$	$+4$	$+4$	$+4$	$+4$	$+4$	$+4$	$+4$
$y = 2x^2 - x + 4$	43	22	9	4	7	18	37

   i Which of Ella's y-values is correct?

   ii Explain what Ella has done wrong.

b This is Pete's table.

Pete's table

x	-3	-2	-1	0	1	2	3
$2x^2$	18	8	2	0	2	8	18
$-x$	-3	-2	-1	0	-1	-2	-3
$+4$	$+4$	$+4$	$+4$	$+4$	$+4$	$+4$	$+4$
$y = 2x^2 - x + 4$	19	10	5	4	5	10	19

   i Which of his y-values are correct?

   ii Explain any mistakes he has made.

 7 a Draw the graph of $y = 5 - 2x - 4x^2$ for $-3 \leqslant x \leqslant +3$

b Use your graph to find the solutions of these equations:

   i $5 - 2x - 4x^2 = 0$ **ii** $5 - 2x - 4x^2 = 4$ **iii** $4x^2 + 2x - 7 = 0$

c Luke says that the equation $5 - 2x - 4x^2 = 9$ cannot be solved.

   i Is he correct?   **ii** Give a reason for your answer.

 8 a Draw the graph of $y = 5x^2 + 2x - 4$ for $-3 \leqslant x \leqslant +3$

b i Write the solutions of the equation $5x^2 + 2x = 4$

   ii Explain how you found the solution and why your method works.

c i Use your graph to solve the equation $30 - 2x = 5x^2$

   ii Explain how you found the solutions and why your method works.

 9 a Draw the graph of $y = 4x(x - 2)$ for values of x from -1 to 3.

b For what value of c does the equation $4x^2 - 8x = c$ have just one solution?

c i Describe the values of c for which the equation $4x^2 - 8x = c$ has no solutions.

   ii Give a reason for your answer.

Explore

Draw the graph of the function $y = ax^2 + bx$ for each set of values of a and b given in this table

Function	a	b	Meets y-axis at	Meets x-axis at	Highest/lowest point
$y = x^2 + 2x$	1	2			
$y = x^2 + 4x$	1	4			
$y = x^2 + 6x$	1	6			
$y = x^2 - 2x$	1	-2			
$y = x^2 - 4x$	1	-4			
$y = x^2 - 6x$	1	-6			
$y = 2x^2 + 2x$	2	2			

Copy and complete the table by entering the coordinates of the points where the curve meets the axes and the coordinates of the highest or lowest point on each curve

Investigate further

Learn 3 Points of intersection of linear and quadratic graphs

Examples:

a i Use a graph to solve the simultaneous equations $y = x^2 + 2x - 4$ and $y = x - 3$

ii How can you tell from the graph that the simultaneous equations $y = x^2 + 2x - 4$ and $y = x - 5$ have no solutions?

i The graph shows the curve $y = x^2 + 2x - 4$ and the line $y = x - 3$

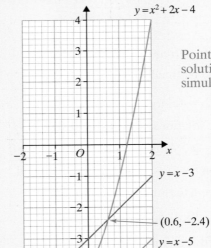

$y = x^2 + 2x - 4$

$y = x - 3$

(0.6, −2.4)

$y = x - 5$

(−1.6, −4.6)

Points of intersection give approximate solutions of the corresponding simultaneous equations

At the points of intersection
$$x^2 + 2x - 4 = x - 3$$
$$x^2 + x - 1 = 0$$

The x-coordinates of the points of intersection are the solutions of this quadratic equation

The solutions are
$$x = -1.6, \qquad y = -4.6$$
and $\quad x = 0.6, \qquad y = -2.4$

The points where the graphs intersect give the solutions of the **simultaneous equations**.

ii The graph of $y = x - 5$ is parallel to $y = x - 3$ but crosses the y-axis at $(0, -5)$.

It does not meet the curve $y = x^2 + 2x - 4$

So the simultaneous equations $y = x^2 + 2x - 4$ and $y = x - 5$ have no solutions.

The graph of a linear function sometimes meets the graph of a quadratic function at two points, sometimes at only one point and sometimes not at all

b i Complete the table values for $y = x^2 - 2x - 2$

x	−2	−1	0	1	2	3	4
y	6	1			−2	1	

ii Draw the graph of $y = x^2 - 2x - 2$ for values of x between −2 and 4.

iii Write down the solutions of $x^2 - 2x - 2 = 0$

iv By drawing an appropriate linear graph write down the solutions of $x^2 - 3x - 1 = 0$

i Completing the table of values for $y = x^2 - 2x - 2$

x	−2	−1	0	1	2	3	4
y	6	1	−2	−3	−2	1	6

ii

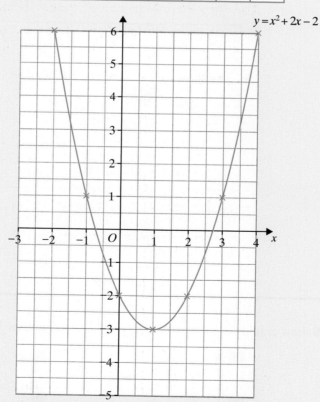

$y = x^2 + 2x - 2$

iii The solutions of $x^2 - 2x - 2 = 0$ are $x = -0.7$ and $x = 2.7$

iv To find the appropriate line:

$$x^2 - 2x - 2 - (x^2 - 3x - 1)$$
$$= x - 1$$

Equation of known line – equation of required line

So we need to draw the line $y = x - 1$

Check:

When $y = x^2 - 2x - 2$ and $y = x - 1$
Then $x^2 - 2x - 2 = x - 1$
$\quad x^2 - 2x - 1 = x$
$\quad x^2 - 3x - 1 = 0$ which is the required equation

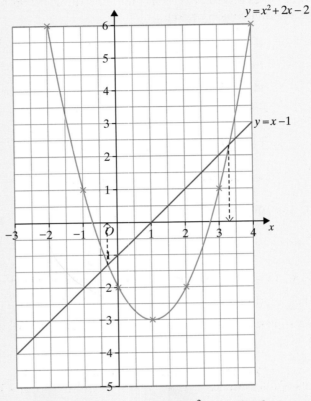

From the graph the solutions of $x^2 - 3x - 1 = 0$ are $x = -0.3$ and $x = 3.3$

Apply 3

In questions **1** to **6** draw graphs for $-4 \leqslant x \leqslant +4$ to solve the simultaneous equations.

1 $y = x + 3$
$\quad y = x^2$

2 $y = 4x$
$\quad y = x^2 + 2$

3 $y = 2x - 4$
$\quad y = -x^2$

4 $x + y = 10$
$\quad y = 3x^2$

5 $y = 5x$
$\quad y = 2x^2 + 1$

6 $x - y + 3 = 0$
$\quad y = 2x(x - 1)$

7 **a** On the same axes draw the graphs of $y = 2 + 4x - x^2$ and $y = x - 1$ for $-1 \leqslant x \leqslant +5$

    b Use your graph to solve the simultaneous equations $y = 2 + 4x - x^2$ and $y = x - 1$

    c Write down and simplify the quadratic equation whose solutions are given by the x-coordinates of the points of intersection of the graphs.

    d How can you tell from the graph that the simultaneous equations $y = 2 + 4x - x^2$ and $y = x + 5$ have no solutions?

8 **a** Draw the graph of $y = 2x^2 - 3x - 2$ for $-1 \leqslant x \leqslant +3$

    b By drawing other lines on your graph, use it to find the solutions of these pairs of simultaneous equations.

      i $y = 2x^2 - 3x - 2$ **ii** $y = 2x^2 - 3x - 2$ **iii** $y = 2x^2 - 3x - 2$
           $y = x - 2$ $y = x - 4$ $y = x - 6$

9 **a** Draw the graph of $y = x^2$ for $-4 \leqslant x \leqslant +4$

    b By drawing other lines on your graph, use it to solve these quadratic equations:

      i $x^2 - 3x = 0$ **ii** $x^2 - x - 5 = 0$ **iii** $x^2 + x - 5 = 0$

    Remember to write down the equations of your other lines.

10 **a** Complete the table of values for $y = x^2 - 2x - 1$

x	−2	−1	0	1	2	3	4
y	7		−1		−1		7

    b Draw the graph of $y = x^2 - 2x - 1$ for values of x between -2 and 4.

    c Write down the solutions of $x^2 - 2x - 1 = 0$

    d By drawing an appropriate linear graph write down the solutions of $x^2 - 3x + 1 = 0$

11 Sam says that you can solve the quadratic equation $2x^2 + 3x - 7 = 0$ by finding the points of intersection of the graphs of $y = 2x^2$ and $y = 3x - 7$ Is he correct? Give a reason for your answer.

12 Work out which graph you would draw on the graph of $y = 5x^2$ to solve each of these equations.

    a $5x^2 - 4x + 1 = 0$

    b $10x^2 - 2x - 3 = 0$

    c $6x - 5x^2 = 7$

    d $x^2 + 3x = 10$

13 Get Real!

A soft drinks manufacturer finds that when they vary the price of a drink, the amount they sell is related to the price by the function $y = 0.01(x - 100)^2$ where x pence is the price per litre and y is the amount sold in thousands of litres per day.

The amount they are willing to make per day is related to the price by $y = 1.5x - 30$ for $x \geqslant 20$.

a Draw a graph showing $y = 0.01(x - 100)^2$ and $y = 1.5x - 30$ for $0 \leqslant x \leqslant 120$

b Explain why the equation $y = 1.5x - 30$ does not apply in this context when $x < 20$.

c Explain why the equation $y = 0.01(x - 100)^2$ is not likely to apply in this context when $x > 100$.

d Write the coordinates of the point of intersection of the graphs and explain the significance of these values in this context.

Explore

◎ Draw the graph of $y = x^2$ for $-3 \leqslant x \leqslant +3$

◎ On the same axes draw the line $y = 2x + 3$

◎ Write the coordinates of the points of intersection of the curve and line

◎ Write a pair of simultaneous equations whose solutions are given by the x-coordinates of the points of intersection of the line and curve

◎ Write down and simplify the quadratic equation whose solutions are given by the x-coordinates of the points of intersection of the line and curve

◎ Repeat the last three steps using the line $y = 2x + 2$

> Investigate further

Quadratic graphs

ASSESS

The following exercise tests your understanding of this chapter, with the questions appearing in order of increasing difficulty.

1 a Taking values of x from -4 to 4, draw tables of values for the functions $y = x^2$, $y = x^2 + 4$ and $y = x^2 - 3$

   b On the same grid, and using the same axes and scales, draw the graphs of these functions.

   c Describe the similarities and differences between the graphs.

2 a Taking values of x from -4 to 4, draw tables of values for the functions $y = x^2$, $y = \frac{1}{2}x^2$ and $y = 3x^2$

   b On the same grid, and using the same axes and scales, draw the graphs of these functions.

   c Describe the similarities and differences between the graphs.

3 a Copy and complete the table of values for the function $y = 2x^2 - 7$

x	−3	−2	−1	0	1	2	3
y	11		−5	−7		1	

b Draw the graph.

c Use your graph to find:

    i the coordinates of the lowest point on the curve

    ii the value of y when $x = 1.4$

    iii the values of x when $y = 6$

    iv the solutions of the equation $2x^2 - 7 = 0$

4 The average safe braking distance for vehicles, d yards, is given by the equation $d = \dfrac{v^2}{50} + \dfrac{v}{3}$, where v is the speed of the vehicle in mph.

a Copy and complete the table of values for the function $d = \dfrac{v^2}{50} + \dfrac{v}{3}$

v (mph)	0	10	20	30	40	50	60	70	80
d (yards)	0	5	15		45	67		121	

b Draw the graph of $d = \dfrac{v^2}{50} + \dfrac{v}{3}$, using v as the horizontal axis.

c Use your graph to find the safe braking distance when the vehicle is travelling at:

    i 15 mph   **ii** 45 mph   **iii** 75 mph.

d A driver suddenly sees an obstruction 50 yards ahead. She just stops in time. How fast was she travelling when she first saw it?

5 a Look at the following method to solve the quadratic equation $y^2 - 2y - 8 = 0$

    Step 1: Rewrite the equation by adding 8 to both sides $y^2 - 2y = 8$

    Step 2: Rewrite the left-hand side as $(y - 1)^2 - 1$ $(y - 1)^2 - 1 = 8$

    Step 3: Tidy up the constants $(y - 1)^2 = 9$

    Step 4: Take the square root of both sides $y - 1 = \pm 3$

    Step 5: Solve the equation $y = 1 \pm 3$ so $y = 4$ or $y = -2$

    i In step 2, why is $(y - 1)$ squared and not $(y - 2)$?

    ii In step 2, why is there −1 after the $(y - 1)^2$?

b Repeat this method to solve these quadratic equations:

    i $x^2 + 2x - 35 = 0$ **iii** $t^2 - 8t + 15 = 0$

    ii $d^2 + 14d + 40 = 0$ **iv** $m^2 - m - 72 = 0$

Try some real past exam questions to test your knowledge:

6 a Complete the table of values for $y = 2x^2 - 4x - 1$

x	−2	−1	0	1	2	3
y	15		−1		−1	5

b Draw the graph of $y = 2x^2 - 4x - 1$ for values of x from −2 to 3.

c An approximate solution of the equation $2x^2 - 4x - 1 = 0$ is $x = 2.2$

   i Explain how you can find this from the graph.

   ii Use your graph to write down another solution of this equation.

Spec A, Higher Paper 1, June 04

7 The grid below shows the graphs of $y = x^2 - x - 6$ and $y = x + 2$

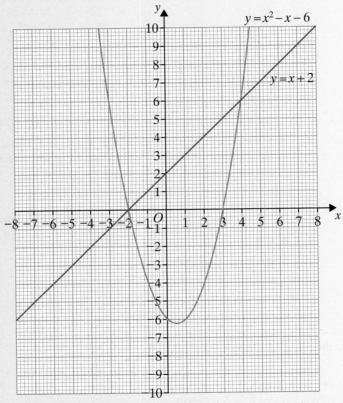

a Deduce the coordinates of the minimum point of the graph $y = x^2 - x - 12$

b Find the quadratic equation whose solutions are the x-coordinates of the points of intersection of $y = x^2 - x - 6$ and $y = x + 2$

Spec A, Higher Paper 2, Nov 03

Glossary

Algebraic expression – a collection of terms separated by + and – signs such as $x + 2y$ or $a^2 + 2ab + b^2$

Amount – the total you will have in the bank or the total you will owe the bank, at the end of the period of time

Balance – the amount of money you have in your bank account or the amount of money you owe after you have paid a deposit

Coefficient – the number (with its sign) in front of the letter representing the unknown, for example:

$4p - 5$ $2 - 3p^2$

4 is the coefficient of p −3 is the coefficient of p^2

Collect like terms – to group together terms of the same variable, for example, $2x + 4x + 3y = 6x + 3y$

Common factor – factors that are in common for two or more numbers, for example,

the factors of 6 are 1, 2, 3, 6
the factors of 9 are 1, 3, 9
the common factors are 1 and 3

Common fraction – see fraction

Compound interest – pays interest on both the original sum and the interest already earned

Consecutive – in sequence

Constant – a number that does not change, for example, the formula $P = 4l$ states that the perimeter of a square is always four times the length of one side; 4 is a constant and P and l are variables

Credit – when you buy goods 'on credit' you do not pay all the cost at once; instead you make a number of payments at regular intervals, often once a month

Cube number – a cube number is the outcome when a whole number is multiplied by itself then multiplied by itself again

Cube root – the cube root of a number such as 125 is a number whose outcome is 125 when multiplied by itself then multiplied by itself again

Decimal – a number in which a decimal point separates the whole number part from the decimal part, for example, 24.8

Decimal fraction – a fraction consisting of tenths, hundredths, thousandths, and so on, expressed in a decimal form, for example, 0.65 (6 tenths and 5 hundredths)

Decimal places – the digits to the right of a decimal point in a number, for example, in the number 23.657, the number 6 is the first decimal place (worth $\frac{6}{10}$), the number 5 is the second decimal place (worth $\frac{5}{100}$) and 7 is the third decimal place (worth $\frac{7}{1000}$); the number 23.657 has 3 decimal places

Degree of accuracy – the accuracy to which a measurement or a number is given, for example, to the nearest 1000, nearest 100, nearest 10, nearest integer, 2 significant figures, 3 decimal places

Denominator – the number on the bottom of a fraction

Deposit – an amount of money you pay towards the cost of an item, with the rest of the cost to be paid later

Depreciation – a reduction in value, for example, due to age or condition

Digit – any of the numerals from 0 to 9

Direct proportion – if two variables are in direct proportion, one is equal to a constant multiple of the other, so that if one increases, the other increases and if one decreases then the other decreases

In general $x \propto y$ and $x = kx$

Discount – a reduction in the price, perhaps for paying in cash or paying early

Equation – a statement showing that two expressions are equal, for example, $2y - 7 = 15$

Equivalent fraction – a fraction that has the same value as another, for example, $\frac{3}{5}$ is equivalent to $\frac{30}{50}, \frac{6}{10}, \frac{60}{100}, \frac{15}{25}, \frac{1.5}{2.5}, \dots$

Estimate – find an approximate value of a calculation; this is usually found by rounding all of the numbers to one significant figure, for example, $\frac{20.4 \times 4.3}{5.2}$ is approximately $\frac{20 \times 4}{5}$ where each number is rounded to 1 s.f.; the answer can be worked out in your head to give 16

Expand – to remove brackets to create an equivalent expression (expanding is the opposite of factorising)

Exponent – see index

Factor – a natural number which divides exactly into another number (no remainder), for example, the factors of 12 are 1, 2, 3, 4, 6 and 12

Factorise – to include brackets by taking common factors (factorising is the opposite of expanding)

Formula – an equation showing the relationship between two or more variables, for example, $E = mc^2$

Fraction or **simple fraction** or **common fraction** or **vulgar fraction** – a number written as one whole number over another, for example, $\frac{3}{8}$ (three eighths), which has the same value as $3 \div 8$

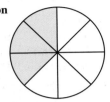

Highest common factor (HCF) – the highest factor that two or more numbers have in common, for example,

the factors of 16 are 1, 2, 4, 8, 16
the factors of 24 are 1, 2, 3, 4, 6, 8, 12, 24
the common factors are 1, 2, 4, 8
the highest common factor is 8

Identity – two expressions linked by the $\equiv$ sign are true for all values of the variable, for example, $3x + 3 \equiv 3(x + 1)$

Improper fraction or **top-heavy fraction** – a fraction in which the numerator is bigger than the denominator, for example, $\frac{13}{5}$, which is equal to the mixed number $2\frac{3}{5}$

Index or **power** or **exponent** – the index tells you how many times the base number is to be multiplied by itself

So $5^3 = 5 \times 5 \times 5$

Index notation – when a product such as $2 \times 2 \times 2 \times 2$ is written as 2^4, the 4 is the index (plural **indices**)

Indices – the plural of index

Integer – any positive or negative whole number or zero, for example, $-2, -1, 0, 1, 2 \ldots$

Interest – money paid to you by a bank, building society or other financial institution if you put your money in an account or the money you pay for borrowing from a bank

Inverse proportion – if two variables are in inverse proportion, their product is a constant; so that if one increases, the other decreases and vice versa

In general $x \propto \frac{1}{y}$ and $x = k\frac{1}{y}$ and $xy = k$

Irrational number – a number that is not an integer and cannot be written as a fraction, for example, $\sqrt{2}, \sqrt{3}, \sqrt{5}$ and π; irrational numbers, when expressed as decimals, are infinite, non-recurring decimals

Least common multiple (LCM) – the lowest multiple which is common to two or more numbers, for example,

the multiples of 3 are 3, 6, 9, 12, 15, 18, 24, 27, 30, 33, 36 …
the multiples of 4 are 4, 8, 12, 16, 20, 24, 28, 32, 36 …
the common multiples are 12, 24, 36 …
the least common multiple is 12

Linear expression – a combination of terms where the highest power of the variable is 1

Linear expressions	Non-linear expressions
x	x^2
$x + 2$	$\frac{1}{x}$
$3x + 2$	$3x^2 + 2$
$3x + 4y$	$(x + 1)(x + 2)$
$2a + 3b + 4c + \ldots$	x^3

Lower bound – this is the minimum possible value of a measurement, for example, if a length is measured as 37 cm correct to the nearest centimetre, the lower bound of the length is 36.5 cm

Mixed number or **mixed fraction** – a number made up of a whole number and a fraction, for example, $2\frac{3}{5}$, which is equal to the improper fraction $\frac{13}{5}$

Multiple – the multiples of a number are the products of its multiplication table, for example, the multiples of 3 are 3, 6, 9, 12, 15 …

Multiplier – a number used to multiply an amount

Numerator – the number on the top of a fraction

Numerator $\longrightarrow \frac{3}{8} \longleftarrow$ Denominator

Percentage – a number of parts per hundred, for example, 15% means $\frac{15}{100}$

Power – see index

Prime factor decomposition – writing a number as the product of its prime factors, for example, $12 = 2^2 \times 3$

Prime number – a natural number with exactly two factors, for example, 2 (factors are 1 and 2), 3 (factors are 1 and 3), 5 (factors are 1 and 5), 7, 11, 13, 17, 23, … 59 …

Principal – the money put into the bank or borrowed from the bank

Product – the result of multiplying together two (or more) numbers, variables, terms or expressions

Proper fraction – a fraction in which the numerator is smaller than the denominator, for example, $\frac{5}{13}$

Proportion – if a class has 12 boys and 18 girls, the proportion of boys in the class is $\frac{12}{30}$, which simplifies to $\frac{2}{5}$, and the proportion of girls is $\frac{18}{30}$, which simplifies to $\frac{3}{5}$ (the **ratio** of boys to girls is $12:18$, which simplifies to $2:3$) – a proportion compares one part with the whole; a ratio compares parts with one another

Quadratic expression – an expression containing terms where the highest power of the variable is 2

Quadratic expressions	Non-quadratic expressions
x^2	x
$x^2 + 2$	$2x$
$3x^2 + 2$	$\frac{1}{x}$
$4 + 4y^2$	$3x^2 + 5x^3$
$(x + 1)(x + 2)$	$x(x + 1)(x + 2)$

Quadratic function – functions like $y = 3x^2$, $y = 9 - x^2$ and $y = 5x^2 + 2x - 4$ are quadratic functions; they include an x^2 term and may also include x terms and constants

The graphs of quadratic functions are always $\cup$-shaped or $\cap$-shaped

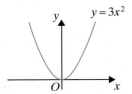

$y = ax^2 + bx + c$ is $\cup$-shaped when a is positive and $\cap$-shaped when a is negative

c is the intercept on the y-axis

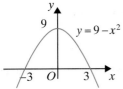

Note that other letters could be used as the variable instead of x (for example, $6t^2 - 3t - 5$ is also a quadratic expression and $h = 30t - 2t^2$ is a quadratic function)

Rate – the percentage at which interest is added, usually expressed as per cent per annum (year)

Ratio – the ratio of two or more numbers or quantities is a way of comparing their sizes, for example, if a school has 25 teachers and 500 students, the ratio of teachers to students is 25 to 500, or $25:500$ (read as 25 to 500)

Rational expression – a fraction, for example,

$$\frac{x^2 - 9}{x + 3}$$

Rational number – a number that can be expressed in the form $\frac{p}{q}$ where p and q are both integers, for example, $1(= \frac{1}{1})$, $2\frac{1}{3}(= \frac{7}{3})$, $\frac{3}{5}$, $0.\dot{1}(= \frac{1}{9})$; rational numbers, when written as decimals, are terminating decimals or recurring decimals

Reciprocal – any number multiplied by its reciprocal equals one; one divided by a number will give its reciprocal, for example, the reciprocal of 3 is $\frac{1}{3}$ because $3 \times \frac{1}{3} = 1$

Recurring decimal – a decimal with a repeating digit or group of digits, for example, 0.33333333333 ... (written as $0.\dot{3}$) or 0.25678678678678 ... (written as $0.25\dot{6}7\dot{8}$)

Round – give an approximate value of a number. Numbers can be rounded to the nearest 1000, nearest 100, nearest 10, nearest integer, significant figures, decimal places ... etc

Significant figures – the digits in a number; the closer a digit is to the beginning of a number then the more important or significant it is; for example, in the number 23.657, 2 is the most significant digit and is worth 20, 7 is the least significant digit and is worth $\frac{7}{1000}$; the number 23.657 has 5 significant digits

Simple fraction – see fraction

Simple interest – pays interest only on the sum of money originally invested

Simplify – to make simpler by collecting like terms

Simplify a fraction or **express a fraction in its simplest form** – to change a fraction to the simplest equivalent fraction; to do this divide the numerator and the denominator by a common factor (this process is called cancelling or reducing or simplifying the fraction)

Square number – a square number is the outcome when a whole number is multiplied by itself

Square root – the square root of a number such as 16 is a number whose outcome is 16 when multiplied by itself

Standard form – standard form is a shorthand way of writing very large and very small numbers; standard form numbers are always written as:

$$A \times 10^n$$

A power of 10

A must be at least 1 but less than 10

Surd – a number containing an irrational root, for example, $\sqrt{2}$ or $3 + 2\sqrt{7}$

Term – a number, variable or the product of a number and a variable(s) such as 3, x or $3x$

Terminating decimal – a decimal that ends, for example, 0.3, 0.33 or 0.3333

Time – usually measured in years for the purpose of working out interest

Top-heavy fraction – see improper fraction

Unitary method – a way of calculating quantities that are in proportion, for example, if 6 items cost £30 and you want to know the cost of 10 items, you can first find the cost of one item by dividing by 6, then find the cost of 10 by multiplying by 10

6 items cost £30

1 item costs $\dfrac{£30}{6}$ = £5

10 items cost 10 × £5 = £50

Unitary ratio – a ratio in the form $1 : n$ or $n : 1$; for example, for every 100 female babies born, 105 male babies are born. The ratio of the number of females to the number of males is 100 : 105; as a unitary ratio, this is 1 : 1.05, which means that, for every female born, 1.05 males are born

Unit fraction – a fraction with a numerator of 1, for example, $\frac{1}{5}$

Upper bound – this is the maximum possible value of a measurement, for example, if a length is measured as 37 cm correct to the nearest centimetre, the upper bound of the length is 37.5 cm

Variable – a symbol representing a quantity that can take different values such as x, y or z

VAT (Value Added Tax) – a tax that has to be added on to the price of goods or services

Vulgar fraction – see fraction